THE RISE OF THE NEW RIGHT

THE RISE OF THE
NEW RIGHT

ALEXANDER MARKOVICS

ARKTOS
LONDON 2026

Copyright © 2026 by Arktos Media Ltd.

All rights reserved. No part of this book may be reproduced or utilised in any form or by any means (whether electronic or mechanical), including photocopying, recording or by any information storage and retrieval system, without permission in writing from the publisher.

ISBN

978-1-918418-23-1 (Paperback)

978-1-918418-24-8 (Hardback)

978-1-918418-25-5 (Ebook)

Translation

Hannah Chernukhina

Editing

Jafe Arnold

Layout and Cover

Tor Westman

Contents

Foreword

by Alexander Raynor

THE TERM 'new right' has been used and abused over the decades by various political movements worldwide. There have been so many 'new right' movements that it is becoming difficult to keep track of them all. However, there is one 'new right' movement that stands above the rest: the European New Right. The European New Right was born in post-war France as the *Nouvelle Droite*. It would then quickly spread throughout the rest of Europe. If you've ever encountered terms or phrases such as "identitarian," "the Great Replacement," or "multipolarity," then you have felt the influence of the European New Right, which would give birth to all these now commonplace political terms we hear coming out of the mouths of TV personalities, podcasters, and even politicians. What separates the European New Right from other 'new rights,' such as those seen in the United States, is its staunch opposition to liberalism, egalitarianism, and individualism. The European New Right views these ideologies as a threat that seeks to eradicate cultural identities. Nowadays, the buzzword *du jour* to describe such threats is "globalism," and even this term itself descends from the *Nouvelle Droite*'s discourse on *mondialisme*. It's remarkable how we've gone from magazines that started out with a circulation of a few hundred people to a political phenomenon that is taking place all over the globe within a few decades. Perhaps you're wondering how we got to this point...

It all started with GRECE, or the Research and Study Group for European Civilization (*Groupement de recherche et d'études pour la civilisation européenne*), founded in 1968, and through its metapolitical strategies that would shape radical-right thought in France and across Europe for decades. The organization's founding was steeped in the principles of metapolitics, a strategy inspired by the Italian Marxist thinker Antonio Gramsci. Metapolitics focuses on influencing cultural and intellectual life to bring about long-term ideological change. In an interview with *Éléments* in 1977, Jean-Claude Valla defined the metapolitical as meaning literally that which comes before—and goes beyond—the political. He defined metapolitics as "the domain of values which do not involve immediate political issues but which act indirectly on the political consensus. To raise the question of politics is to raise the question of ideology. In our sense of the word, 'ideology' is the mental system which results from the manner in which the world is perceived and acted upon. Historically, it is the putting into practice of ideology which constitutes culture."[1] Gramscianism, or metapolitics, is designed to awaken certain individuals, namely, intellectual, political, and economic elites, to new ways of seeing and being, to change hearts and minds, and to gain support for alternative, counter-hegemonic conceptions of the world. GRECE's efforts were concentrated on promoting ideas through publications, seminars, and collaborations with thinkers across Europe. This approach sought to establish a "new culture" as a foundation for a "new right" (a title cast upon them by the media), distinct from traditional conservative movements. Nowadays, when you look at the political landscape, you can see all kinds of organizations, journals, publishing houses, and e-personalities knowingly (or unknowingly)

---

1   The interview was conducted with Jean-Claude Valla in 1977 and comprises the second chapter of *"Pour une renaissance culturelle"* (For a Cultural Renaissance), titled "A Community of Work and Thought." An English translation is available on *European New Right Revue*: https://nouvelledroite.substack.com/p/a-community-of-work-and-thought.

engaging with the concept of metapolitics. You can also see the resurgence in popularity of certain political thinkers, such as Carl Schmitt, Vilfredo Pareto, James Burnham, and Samuel Francis, who take a more *realpolitik* or Machiavellian approach to political power and the elites. This is all metapolitics. If you cannot become one of the elites, then perhaps you can change the hearts and minds of the elites. As the old saying goes, "if you can't beat them, join them" (or in this case, get them to join you).

We cannot discuss the *Nouvelle Droite* without mentioning its chief architect, Alain de Benoist. De Benoist embodies the core values of GRECE and the *Nouvelle Droite*. De Benoist has written dozens of books, hundreds of articles, and granted just as many interviews over several decades of metapolitical activism. This is not to discount the influence and importance of other thinkers involved in the *Nouvelle Droite*, such as Guillaume Faye, Pierre Vial, Robert Steuckers, and Tomislav Sunic, but Alain de Benoist is the key figure of the movement. From his leadership in GRECE, all other strains of thought are inspired, such as Vial's identitarianism, Faye's archeofuturism, and Alexander Dugin's Fourth Political Theory. I say that as someone deeply inspired by Guillaume Faye's work. While de Benoist would never ascribe such labels as identitarian or Eurasianist to himself, he has served as a spiritual godfather of sorts to many ideological and political movements over the past several decades.

GRECE, under the leadership of Alain de Benoist, has held over 20 conferences and founded three major journals that remain in circulation to this day (*Éléments*, *Nouvelle École*, and *Krisis*). Countless books have been written by all of the thinkers, journalists, and activists who comprise the movement. As they say, imitation is the sincerest form of flattery, and GRECE has inspired similar metapolitical organizations worldwide. Nowadays, the torchbearer of European New Right thought and metapolitical activism is the Iliade Institute. The creation of the Iliade Institute was the final wish of Dominique Venner before he took his life at Notre Dame Cathedral on May 21st,

2013, in a final act of protest against the Great Replacement. Several of the children of the old guard are key figures at the Iliade Institute, including Dominique's son, Guillaume, and Pierluigi Locchi (son of the great Italian thinker Giorgio Locchi). The Iliade Institute holds annual conferences, offers training seminars for activists, and publishes books. Thus, the anti-liberal, pro-European tradition continues after more than fifty years of intensive and extensive propagation.

Just as that tradition has persisted in France for over half a century, it has persisted in other European countries as well, such as with Michael Walker and *Scorpion* (England), Marco Tarchi (Italy), Pierre Krebs (Germany), Robert Steuckers (Belgium), *Elementos* (Spain), and Marcel Rüter (Holland). France takes most of the credit for birthing the European New Right, hogging all the spotlight, but it is now truly a European-wide phenomenon. The anti-liberal, pro-European New Right tradition continues in the German-speaking world as the *Neue Rechte*, pioneered by thinkers and activists such as Armin Mohler, Pierre Krebs, Martin Sellner, and the author of the book you are currently reading, Alexander Markovics. Markovics is an individual I have known for quite some time. As mentioned previously, de Benoist has been the spiritual godfather to many movements; in this case, he would inspire Markovics to become one of the founding fathers of *Identitäre Bewegung Österreich* (Generation Identity Austria). It was a surprise and an honor that Markovics reached out to me to write the foreword for his book. As a historian and translator of the *Nouvelle Droite*, I have encountered many outsider perspectives who attempt to examine and understand the European New Right, but most miss the mark or have ulterior motives to lambast the movement, to brand it as "neo-fascist" or "racist." On the other hand, Markovics is a man deeply steeped in the philosophy of the European New Right, having been an activist, journalist, theoretician, and writer within it for many years.

Through the topography of the European New Right which Markovics presents here, it becomes clear that the European New

Right is alive and well, continuing to grow, expand, and evolve, much like Markovics himself. Having initially started in identitarianism, Markovics has since pivoted to Eurasianism and Dugin's Fourth Political Theory—which I would describe as an intellectual strain of thought that is not of the *Nouvelle Droite* but is clearly inspired by it. Dugin himself was the Russian correspondent for *Éléments* back in the early 1990s, founded a Russian-language version named *Elementy*, and even put together an anthology of Alain de Benoist's essays in a book titled *Against Liberalism: Towards a Fourth Political Theory*. Dugin has borrowed heavily from the *Nouvelle Droite* itself and other intellectual traditions that have inspired the European New Right (such as the Traditionalism of René Guénon and Julius Evola, the philosophy of Martin Heidegger, and the thinkers of the German Conservative Revolution), forged his own philosophical theory, and presented it from a Russian perspective. One could say that the European New Right is the spiritual godfather of the Fourth Political Theory and Eurasianism. Markovics is currently the editor of the German journal *Agora Europa*, a metapolitical publication which combines European New Right and Eurasianist thought.

Markovics's *The Rise of the New Right* is exactly what the discourse surrounding this movement has long needed: a meticulously researched, rigorously argued, and intellectually serious examination of one of Europe's most misunderstood currents of thought. His book provides an excellent overview of the thinkers, organizations, and strains of thought that have shaped the European New Right over the past half-century, continue to shape it presently, and will continue to shape it going forward.

Foreword to the German Edition

by Marian Penkö

A s I was pondering how I should begin this preface, the Hanau shootings of 2020 took place. The establishment media immediately instrumentalized the event in a bid to vilify the movements of the New Right, even before the mental condition of the perpetrator was known. The leftist media framed it as the apex of a plague of "politically self-conscious right-wing violence." Then, as always happens, these commenters seemed to immediately arrive at the cause of this plague, as well as its obvious cure (more resources for the "fight against the right"). But nobody inquired into the actual social and spiritual conditions that might have incited such an act of violence.

In 1870, in his notions of the "Death of God" and our collective fall into a "World Night" (German: *Weltnacht*), Friedrich Nietzsche foresaw a calamity which has since come to pass. Yet the nihilism of modernity has dared to aggravate itself even further in the era of postmodernity. The best expression of this next phase is to be found in Zygmunt Bauman's *Postmodernity and Its Discontents*. It takes every other grand narrative to the grave, in addition to that of God: it abolishes the notion of an organic community through the corrosive effects of individualism and the arbitrary values of liberalism; it liquidates the socium and the solidarity of neighbors by dragging the youth out of the countryside and into the anonymity of the cities; it dissolves local traditions by means of an all-encompassing, global standardization; and it voids all possibility of myth through the materialization of values into commodities. However, one easily forgets that these phenomena, including Western egalitarianism, all share the same root: liberalism.

The negative repercussions of postmodernity on the spiritual health of Europeans have not gone unnoticed by their leftist, egalitarian advocates. They have found themselves, not without reason, in a defensive position for some time now, whose rallying point and final redoubt is constituted by the ideology of human rights. The heavy losses of the social democrats in Germany and Austria during the most recent elections are illustrative examples. The populistic currents — at least those which have manifested in Austria — seem to have been more successful; certain forms of neoconservatism bearing the marks of having been influenced by the ideas of Egon Flaig's *Defeat of Political Reason* (*Niederlage der politischen Vernunft*) have proven equally popular. The implications for the civilizational and philosophical developments of Europe over the last several centuries are made clear in the subtitle of Flaig's book: *How We Squander the Achievements of the Enlightenment* (*Wie wir die Errungenschaften der Aufklärung verspielen*).

More notable still is the thought of sociologist Andreas Reckwitz, who fears the end of the narrative of liberal progress — that grand narrative which has been so exhaustively propagated and internalized in the West. Because Francis Fukuyama's *End of History* has proven erroneous, the expectations placed upon the liberal narrative of progress must inevitably now go unfulfilled. What has arisen is disillusionment which, incidentally, is the reason for the popularity of Egon Flaig's Christian-Western universalism and the transformation of the old major "people's parties" ("new conservatism") as they reacted to the same exact causes. The egalitarian Left does not understand this, however. The "project of modernity" ought ultimately to have brought gains and improvements through "liberalization." As Reckwitz writes in his book *The End of Illusions* (Germ. *Das Ende der Illusionen*), the ultimate fruits of liberalism in the West have proved to be nothing more than hedonism and cosmopolitanism. In this context, he refers not only to the artificial character of modernity, which he recognizes to have been a concentrated effort to transform society, but also to the New Right. The signs of decline he describes "are enormously present in the media." It is these and other symptoms which have rendered Spengler's cyclical philosophy of history relevant once more. For proponents of the fundamentally linear ideology of progress (as critiqued by Alain de Benoist), such developments are understandably horrifying.

In fact, the driving agents of the egalitarianism which has caused the erosion of collective identities have always been a subject and target of criticism for the *Nouvelle Droite*. Instead of listing the morbidities of the currently rotting European corpse, I could instead have just as well begun by quoting the table of contents of any work by Alain de Benoist. Several months before the May 1968 student protests in France, de Benoist was in Nice alongside the other founding members of GRECE (Fr. *Groupement de recherche et d'études pour la civilisation européenne*; The Research and Study Group for European Civilization). It is therefore only logical that we understand the *Nouvelle Droite* not as a reaction to the New Left, but as an entirely different orientation. We must pay special attention to the origins and pre-history of this school of thought. The urgency of this consideration is only made greater by the flak which de Benoist and his ideas have received in Germany since 2010. Repeating, in a rather curious way, the Mohler-Molnar controversy of 1978,[1] the neoconservatives attacked the New Right and attached compromising labels to their ideas in a bid to disable them; as a result, the *Nouvelle Droite* went into a temporary dormancy. The fact that Götz Kubitschek later launched the Identitarian Movement in the journal *Provokation,*

---

1   The debate between Armin Mohler and Thomas Molnar was published in the German conservative journal *Criticon* (issue 47/3, 1978) under the title "Debate between the Two Conservative Schools of Thought" ("*Streitgespräch zwischen den beiden konservativen Denkschulen*").

treating it as an activist outlet of the New Right only to be buried in short order, is sufficient to exhibit the irony of cycles.

Nevertheless, the right-wing intelligentsia in Germany inevitably took the side of the political realists in the likes of Thomas Molnar and the neoconservatives, who have never understood, nor wished to understand, this all-out offensive against liberalism. However, one ought to differentiate between cultural and economic liberalism — so goes the common dogma. Likewise, one often hears that the term "neoliberalism" is actually a misnomer, assertive of nothing. At the same time, neoliberalism has recently come under stiff attack in the course of heated debates over climate issues.[2] In light of this, one is tempted to ask whether the subject of public criticism has been conceptually adequate, or whether it has been incorrectly formulated. This question was unintentionally answered by the liberal philosopher Felix Pinkert, who has posited that the neoliberalism exemplified by Trump's protectionism and the popular flirtation with strong statehood presently finds itself in retreat, and is nothing other than an atrophied form of liberalism.

Liberalism admittedly affects all aspects of life. To clarify further, "a strong people (German: *Volk*) contradicts the idea of the liberated and strong individual."[3] The *Nouvelle Droite* constitutes the single remaining intellectual current that has declared liberalism to be its main enemy; furthermore, only the *Nouvelle Droite* is launching concrete attacks against it. The author of the present work, Alexander Markovics, places the greatest emphasis on this fact.

Yet, we must also acknowledge the New Right's concern with ecology and climate change. While contemporary philosophers such as Pinkert argue that neoliberalism is not responsible for climate

---

2   Aloysius Widmann, "Bedeutet die Klimakrise das Aus für den Neoliberalismus? Eine Analyse und ein Interview mit dem Politexperten Colin Crouch," *Der Standard* (29.02.2020) [https://www.pressreader.com/austria/der-standard/20200229/282754883741616].

3   Felix Pinkert, quoted in ibid.

change, but rather its solution, Alain de Benoist has previously put forth a critique to the contrary, namely that the great global challenges — global warming chief among them — cannot be addressed as long as discussions concerning such issues take place within the fixed framework of infinite growth.

The New Right is equally concerned with geopolitical matters. During the Munich Security Conference of February 2020, the United States launched an overt verbal attack on China, following broadsides from the Chinese. The press commented on the incident in the context of the "courting of Europe," stating that, in this chaotic world situation, Europe was striving "for self-determination."[4] This is a remarkable statement, and such talk of a self-determined Europe which should adopt a geopolitically self-sufficient, militarily strengthened position has already been given voice by the highest representative of the European Commission in Austria, Martin Selmayr, who has taken up office in Vienna.

That this "idea" should emerge only after the United States and China had threatened to pulverize Europe with trade and information wars should surprise connoisseurs of the *Nouvelle Droite,* who, already for some time, have understood Europe to be a strong "middle-realm." Even before the collapse of the Soviet Union, it was Alain de Benoist who had warned of American hegemony — not because he had grown tired of the right-wing railing against the peril of communism, but because it was intent on preventing an eventual multipolar world order. Through his partisanship for a strong, federally structured Europe as a middle-realm, de Benoist built upon Ernst Jünger's 1946 proposition of a federalized Europe.

These pluralistic deliberations have been expanded by Alexander Dugin. In *The Fourth Political Theory,* Dugin has further developed the concept of a "multipolar world," recognizing that a strengthened

---

4   "Der globale Siegeszug der autoritären Systeme," *Die Presse* (15.03.2021) [https://www.diepresse.com/5951194/der-globale-siegeszug-der-autoritaeren-systeme].

multipolar order amounts to a rejection of the universality of Western civilization.[5] We effectively find ourselves living in the liberal sphere of the "West," under American cultural and cognitive hegemony, whose liberalism we largely continue to leave unquestioned. Unlike Andreas Reckwitz, Alexander Dugin sees all too well how liberalism has been the victorious result of modernity. However, it remains to be seen whether liberalism, the first political theory of modernity, will be the last one standing. If Reckwitz's "End of Illusions"[6] means the collapse of liberalism, and if our subsequent disillusionment is to be understood as a rejection of the "one world" model, this is certainly an opportunity for the peoples of Europe. Along with Dugin, we must recognize that postmodernity is under no circumstances our fate.

Alexander Markovics is an outstanding authority on the theory of the *Nouvelle Droite*, having taken part in the Identitarian movement from its beginning. After withdrawing therefrom, Markovics has occupied himself with the theory of the New Right and its geopolitics, hosting reading groups and giving lectures across Europe. The present book draws heavily on manuscript material that has been accumulated over the years. That these materials have now taken form as an introduction to the New Right pleases me particularly.

Marian Penkö
Vienna, March 2020

---

5 Alexander Dugin, *The Fourth Political Theory* (London: Arktos, 2012).

6 Andreas Reckwitz, *Das Ende der Illusionen. Politik, Ökonomie und Kultur* (Berlin: Suhrkamp, 2019). In English: Andreas Reckwitz, *The End of Illusions: Politics, Economy, and Culture in Late Modernity* (Cambridge: Polity, 2021).

Introduction

A SPECTER IS haunting Europe. However, it is not the ghost of communism. It is the New Right that is now managing to strike fear, time after time, into the hearts of the liberal elite. In the scaremongering driven by mainstream media around the rise of populist movements, everything gets labeled with the tag "New Right," from carriers of anti-Islamist ideas to libertarians who wish to reduce the state to an absolute minimum. The rise of right-wing populistic parties in Germany and Europe is interpreted as the rise of a "New Right," in a similar manner to how patriotic publishing houses are marked as pariahs by the "liberal-democratic constitutional order." This is not conducive to a clear delineation and denomination of ideological currents. On the contrary, it leads to a willful tumult and disarray of concepts, and even as far as to accusations of extremism, which are calculated so as to socially isolate and silence supporters and sympathizers. To throw schools and movements of oppositional thought into the same pot as loud-mouthed extremists, and to criminalize the thought of both, remains from time immemorial the standard praxis for maintaining power. However, with all of this fearmongering about the "New Right" (as per Thomas Wagner[1]), one question remains unanswered: what actually is the New Right? Is it a new

---

1 Thomas Wagner (b. 1967) is a German Sociologist associated with the German communist newspaper *Junge Welt*. In his book *Die Angstmacher. 1968 und die Neuen Rechten* (Berlin: Aufbau Verlag, 2017), he broke the taboo on isolating the New Right and engaged in discussion with the "fearmongers" of the New Right. See also his *Robokratie. Google, das Silicon Valley und der Mensch als Auslaufmodell* (Cologne: Papyrossa Verlag, 2015).

school of thought with revolutionary aspirations which has set about to overcome old thought patterns? Or is it merely expired goods in a new package, a more intellectually elevated National Socialism, as the liberal-Marxist "anti-fascists" claim?

This book will address such issues and, in doing so, will put an end to the turbulence of concepts surrounding the New Right and its associated labels. This text is therefore conceived as an introduction to the New Right. On the one hand, it is meant to provide newcomers with an overview of the origins and themes of the New Right, its most prominent thinkers, ideas, and actors; on the other hand, it will serve those already familiar with this school of thought as a refresher, perhaps even deepening their grasp of the subject. In this regard, the book at hand is not a comprehensive exposition of the thinkers and concepts belonging to the New Right, but rather is a curated primer. This book covers the broad outlines of the New Right, from its beginnings in France up to today. It does not address more recent developments, such as the "Alt-Right" phenomenon of the mid-to-late 2010s. Anyone searching for an exhaustive account of all the phenomena which have ended up under the label of the "New Right," but which are ultimately the old ideologies of modernity in new garments, will not find what they are looking for here.

However, anyone looking for radical ideas that might lead to Europe's rebirth — that might unify and embody both left-wing and right-wing methods for the sake of overcoming post-modernity and reconnecting to European tradition — will find exactly what they are looking for.

The first section of the book focuses on the early history of the New Right and its intellectual pioneers: Dominique Venner and Jean-François Thiriart, leaders of the National-Revolutionary Right after the Second World War. Our reference to these two figures will double as an analysis of transformations in the Right's intellectual history, particularly with regard to the developments of the 20th century. Here, we consider the fault lines out of which a new kind of thinking emerged, set in stark contrast to the dominant currents of right-wing thought that had preceded the war. Firstly, this involves the story of Jean-François Thiriart and his experience in the Second World War, which has been perceived by many National-Revolutionaries as a "European civil war." This murderous conflict led not only to the end of Europe as an independent geopolitical unit, but also to its partition between an American-dominated West and a Soviet-dominated East. The resultant feeling of impotence among Europeans had a cathartic impact on some representatives of the Right, who had been forced into a state of self-reflection on the heels of internecine strife and racial fanaticism, and who now advocated for a united Europe that could overcome the dilemma of nation-states. After all, lone nations would be helpless in the face of the dual hegemonies of the US and the USSR. Secondly, the experience of Dominique Venner is revealing, given that he personally witnessed not only the loss of European power in his time, but also the failed coup against French President Charles de Gaulle. This attempted coup revealed the flaws of the "Old Right," as well as its total lack of strategy. Venner's participation therein landed him behind bars. Yet, instead of resigning himself and bemoaning the past, during his imprisonment he undertook to analyze the Old Right and to deliberate on the question of transforming the disorganized right-wing in France and Europe into a revolutionary and formidable pan-European force. Based on this episode, we can ascertain why dissident forces within the French Right went their own way, avoiding the path of a "Fascism without the Führer," a path which many others on the Right took throughout Europe.

The second section is dedicated to the birth of the New Right, starting from the founding of GRECE (*Groupement de recherche et d'études pour la civilisation européenne*; The Research and Study Group for European Civilization) around Alain de Benoist prior to the summer of protests of 1968. We engage extensively with its ideas, from the concept of "Cultural Revolution from the Right" to the rediscovery of metapolitics. As part of this exhibit of ideas, broader concepts known to the public, such as ethnopluralism, are also discussed, as are the hot potatoes, such as the stirring notion of the "Great Replacement" which re-entered public consciousness after the mosque attack in Christchurch, New Zealand. Right-wing readers will find a number of unfamiliar and perhaps even controversial approaches here, such as the New Right's anti-capitalist position, its concern with environmental conservation and growth decline, as well as its views on Islam, the nation-state, the bourgeoisie, and populism. These subjects may admittedly induce a certain discombobulation in the right-wing reader upon first engaging with them — but, if so, this only goes to illustrate the fundamental differences between the Old and New Rights. What is essential here is liberalism's status as the primary enemy — the barricade separating the New Right from the "Davos people" (Samuel Huntington). By this latter camp, we mean those right-wing movements that combine support for the free-market economy with a merely conservative flavoring of liberalism.

The New Right holds to a vision which rejects egoism and individualism and upholds the ideal of community and communitarianism. Its basic idea is connected to the Platonic concept of a cultural war of metapolitics which not only precedes party politics, but reduces the latter to a mere executive organ within an organism. This gesture of the New Right should be understood as a rallying cry, a call to return to focusing on ideas and ceasing to see parliaments as a panacea. It also concerns the question of geopolitics, which the New Right, in the spirit of Carl Schmitt, does not repudiate, but instead recognizes to be an important dimension of the Political (*das Politische*). In this respect, the New Right professes hostility towards the hegemonic United States, which tries to impose its values of democracy and human rights on everyone in the world, transforming the world into a universe that knows only one end of history. Instead, the New Right advocates a multipolar world, divided into great spaces (*Grossraum*), in which Europe will once more find Her own borders, liberate Herself from liberal universalism, and fulfill Her role as the *Katekhon* anew, after having relinquished it at the end of the Middle Ages.

This plea for a continuation of history leads us, last but not least, to philosophy. The Russian New Right associated with Neo-Eurasianism has, through its most prominent exponent, Alexander Dugin, engaged with philosophical ideas and the search for *Dasein*.[2] Alongside Alain de Benoist, who remains the most important representative of the French New Right, Dugin's work constitutes a milestone in the development of New Right thought. Based on his conception of the Fourth Political Theory, which places *Dasein* at its center as it seeks to overcome modernity, he proposes the beginnings of an alternative to liberalism. Among Dugin's influences are the two Traditionalists, René Guénon and Julius Evola, the latter also having been closely associated with the German Conservative Revolution (*Konservative Revolution*) movement. But an even greater influence on him has come from the philosophy of Martin Heidegger. These forebears' ideas ultimately lead Dugin to postulate an alternative not only to liberalism, but to modernity itself. The discipline of ethnosociology in which Dugin engages follows precisely in this direction, asking what the *ethnos* or the people (Russian: народ) really is, refuting the modern logic which necessitates a worldwide civil society after the bourgeois nation-state has run its course. In his *magnum opus, Noomakhia*, he analyzes the war that rages all around us, the war which we hear in the subtitle of the work: "Wars of the Mind" (войны ума). In doing so, he further expands on the ideas of Friedrich Nietzsche and Martin Heidegger, discovering, alongside the Logos of Apollo and Logos of Dionysus, the Logos of Cybele. Nevertheless, this civilization, stamped by the materialism and matriarchy of the Great Mother is not dead. Rather, according to Dugin, Europe has established itself through the conquest of the proto-European space carried out by the Indo-Europeans and

---

2 See Martin Heidegger's *Sein und Zeit* [*Being and Time*].

through its superimposition of the old, Cybelean form with the newer Apollonian one. The result of this combination was the Dionysian Logos, yet the Cybelean structures were not thereby destroyed; they remained dormant, preserved in European peasantry. The Cybelean Logos only reemerged at the end of the Middle Ages, as modernity was dawning, along with its "natural science," "humanism," and capitalism.

In summary, the major representatives and ideas of the French, Scandinavian, and German New Right are presented in detail here, laying the groundwork for a comprehensive introduction to the heritage and perspectives of the New Right. My special thanks go to the publishing house Arcadi for first making the launch of this book in German possible, as well as Marian Penkö for his collaboration in the Viennese reading circle of the New Right, to say nothing of his long-lasting friendship and kindness, which contributed to deepening and expanding the present book's contents. Finally, I would like to express my gratitude to Arktos and its editor-in-chief, Jafe Arnold, for the present English edition, which is now more up to date than the German thanks to the tireless efforts of him and his team.

ALEXANDER MARKOVICS

Vienna,

February 2026

A Rebellious Heart: Dominique Venner and the Positive Critique of the Old Right

THE PRELUDE to the New Right took place in Western Europe. Following the Second World War, France was a country under reconstruction. Once more, representative democracy governed. The Fourth Republic had emerged, and it would prove to be chronically unstable during the Cold War. Meanwhile, the French Communist Party had become the strongest of its kind in Europe, in part thanks to its partisan actions against the German occupation at its peak. But the Communists were kept out of power by the Gaullists and Christian Democrats. After the fall of the *État français* and the Vichy Regime (1940–1944), the French Republic remained a largely agrarian country, whose peasantry constituted more than one third of the populace. While the economy vigorously recovered during the "Glorious Thirties" (*Les Trente Glorieuses*) and the consumer society gradually began to emerge, the Republic was facing a humiliating defeat in Vietnam, having been routed at Diên Biên Phu in 1954. But, though the war in Vietnam had merely been a far-flung escapade in Southeast Asia, the eruption of the Algerian War (1954–1962) hit much closer to home, triggered as it was by the murder of French teachers.

We should first note that Algeria was not a colony in the classical sense at that time. Officially, it was an immediate part of the French motherland. Like the Anglo-Saxon colonies which had been established in North America, Australia, and New Zealand, the Algerian territories occupied in 1830 began as a settlement colony, where 1.4

million ethnic French were already living at the outbreak of the war; these were the so-called *Pieds-Noirs* ("Black Feet"). Secondly, for the French back home, it was not obvious whose side they ought to take. While the nationalist youth came out in rabid defense of French Algeria (*Algérie Française*), the Communist Party agitated alongside the reinforced Left for an end to the French presence there.

The young Dominique Venner (1935–2013) belonged to the first group. He saw those events as a means of escape from the seemingly stifling life of France.[1] Coming straight from the elite military school Rouffach in Alsace,[2] Venner spent the war performing guard duties and reconnaissance patrols against the Algerian National Liberation Front. This guerrilla force tended to avoid open battle against the French Army. However, while the troops were fighting in the field, the Communist youth were protesting in France against the war. Supported by Marxist intellectuals such as Jean-Paul Sartre (1905–1980),[3] who wished to make up for his lack of commitment in the *Résistance* (1940–1944), voices like those of Frantz Fanon struck the hearts of the suppressed colonial peoples, but also questioned the meaning of republican France. Epitomized by the war hero and president, Charles de Gaulle (1890–1970), most of the French at the time were more interested in increasing their own wellbeing than in the preservation of the French colonial empire. So, it happened that the war was being led by a widely defeatist society and, however cruel the war, its battles were brief and claimed few lives.[4]

When Dominique Venner had enough of the French Army's defeatism, and of journalists loudly opposing the war in Algeria, and could no longer ignore the atrocities which had been committed by the National Liberation Front (*Front de Libération Nationale*, FLN),

---

1   Alain de Benoist, foreword to Dominique Venner, *Das rebellische Herz* (Jungeuropa, 2018), 8.

2   Dominique Venner, *Das rebellische Herz*, 39.

3   Ibid., 26.

4   Ibid., 28.

he decided to join the OAS (*Organisation Armée Secrète*, The Secret Army Organization). This organization sought to turn the tide of the war by means of terror attacks in the motherland and even an attack on de Gaulle. However, personal infighting, human failure, dilettantism, the lack of a far-reaching strategy, and state repression had paralyzed the revolts around General Raoul Salan (1899–1984).[5] The war eventually ended disastrously for the *Pieds Noirs*, the French Right, and Dominique Venner: more than one million Frenchmen were forced to flee across the Mediterranean to France. The end of the war found Venner in prison and the Right demoralized.

Yet, instead of collapsing into self-pity and seeking excuses for his personal failures, Venner began not only to learn from them, but also to critically reflect on his actions. In the makeshift academy that was *La Santé* detention center, Venner grappled above all with French nationalism and its deficiencies.[6] At the end of these contemplations, in 1962, he published his book *Towards a Positive Critique* [*Pour une critique positive*]. In light of the failure of the OAS, Venner begins his work by listing the deficiencies of the National Opposition. Inspired by Lenin's work *What is to Be Done?* (*Что делать?*), he criticizes an idea that many nationalists harbour, namely that a revolution should be something spontaneous that breaks out without any premeditation. The great significance of this work lies in its differentiation between the "nationals," by which Venner means France's Old Right, and the "nationalists," by which he means those nationalist revolutionaries who emerged reformed after the disastrous coup against de Gaulle. Then, Venner begins his post-mortem of the Old Right, critiquing their idea of revolution. According to Venner, revolutions are not spontaneous; moreover, they demand a clear worldview (*Weltanschauung*) which clarifies contemporary deficiencies, such as the causes for Western decadence, all in order to steer activism

---

5   Ibid., 60.

6   Benedikt Kaiser, "Wer war Dominique Venner?" in Dominique Venner, *Für eine positive Kritik* (Dresden: Jungeuropa Verlag, 2017), 8.

into ordered lanes. A major characteristic of the "nationals" (whom he presents as a caricature of the ideologically conscious nationalist revolutionaries) is their constant failure, because they never attack anything more than the fruits of evil, without ever directly uprooting it. So, while they were fanatical anti-communists, they also turned a blind eye to the ravages of capitalism and liberalism — the two predecessors to communism. Another flaw of the "nationals" is their conformism. Any bourgeois politician swinging a national flag is capable of deceiving them because, when it comes to the Political (*das Politische*), even they are dominated by sentimentality and superficial thinking.[7]

The national opposition's second major shortcoming, according to Venner, is its deficiency in organizing its own actions, which stems predominantly from its lack of ideas within the domain of political struggle. A side-effect of this is ultimately the rampant opportunism that comes from the ambition of individual MPs. They deceive themselves that they can acquire a position in the liberal regime, and hence always only direct their criticism against a politician or a government because of their wish to avoid addressing the essence of the matter, or questioning the regime *per se*. Once the winds turn, these people are the first to betray their own supporters, in order to save their own skin.[8] On this point, Venner presents a fundamental critique of parliamentarism. A seat in parliament is not a means of struggle, but rather only an end that must be preserved at any cost. The simple followers of right-wing parties, on the other hand, are opportunists, since they lack not only a worldview, but also any training to speak of. They would rather give lauded speeches and seek to make a superficial impression than analyze political ideas and circumstances in any substantial sense. Therefore, they are doomed to deception. Venner identifies a further weakness in their fixation on myth. By

---

7   Dominique Venner, *Für eine positive Kritik*, 27. In English: Dominique Venner, *For a Positive Critique* (London: Arktos, 2017).

8   Ibid., 28.

myth, he does not mean the need for one great mobilising narrative, but the tendency towards conspiratorial methods; constantly, they brandish their *liaisons* with individual members of the government as a sign that the regime is soon to topple.[9]

Terrorism on the part of the Right always results from an erroneous analysis of the situation and from the shortcomings of their worldview. While some ultimately succumb to opportunism due to their ideological shortcomings, others choose the route of attacks and systemic violence against civilians. Venner regards blind terrorism as the easiest way to lose the support of the population.[10] Violence and conspiratorial actions, Venner claims, would only be useful to a nation after it had depleted all other available means in seeking justice. In the past, terrorists had always aimed to mobilize people for their own struggle against a perceived exterior enemy. But whoever employs it against his own population must necessarily fail, explains Venner. A further error arises from the "nationals'" predilection towards anarchy. The "nationals" indeed admire discipline, but are nonetheless incapable of organizing themselves within an ordered structure. They tend to act in an uncoordinated manner and to ignore any guidelines set out for them, rendering them powerless to concentrate their forces. The result of this anarchistic mentality is ultimately the Right's fragmentation.[11] In his plea for the development of a revolutionary theory, Venner insists that, before a reform of the national faction is possible, it must be subjected to a fundamental critique. Of course, he argues that one cannot understand this if one lacks political maturity. In this context, revolution is to be understood not as a seizure of power, but as an application of power towards building a new society.[12] Considering the strength

---

9   Ibid., 29.

10   Ibid., 65ff.

11   Ibid., 30.

12   Ibid., 31.

of contemporary states, the idea of a sudden uprising which would usher in radical changes is a relic of the past. Contrary to conditions during the interwar period, states nowadays boast a strong police apparatus as well as a technocracy at all levers of power who have captured the leading positions in politics, the economy, and governmental administrations. With the state controlling the minds of its citizens, they are rendered docile sheep. With no leader in sight, the revolutionary Right must be able to rely on every one of its members, as though they were players on a football team.[13] Nevertheless, in order to generate a revolution, one must first cultivate a revolutionary awareness. For this purpose, one must understand how the liberal regime functions, expose its methods, and unmask its accomplices — especially those who try to pass themselves off as "patriots." The realization of revolutionary awareness demands an exhaustive interrogation of modernity's "established truths."

At this point, Dominique Venner describes his inclinations in more detail: the revolutionary must be completely aware of the struggle between Western nationalism and materialism, both in its liberal and Marxist forms.[14] Accordingly, prioritizing the formation of future cadres is critically important, as even the bravest and most daring man is nothing more than a "manipulated puppet of the regime" without this formative nationalist-revolutionary education. This is particularly necessary due to the unilateral and uninterrupted propaganda of the regime that has enjoyed a monopoly over the people and poisoned their minds. This propaganda attacks every critical mind and thought in democratic regimes.[15] The revolutionary struggle is to be understood as a psychological struggle, urges Venner. Within this framework, one must harness the enthusiasm of his followers. This necessarily requires a comprehensible doctrine, capable of awakening

---

13 Ibid., 32ff.

14 Ibid., 34.

15 Ibid., 35.

their fighting spirit and accessibly conveying its doctrine to the hesitant. An agreement on common action cannot last without a common underlying doctrine. It is therefore imperative, Venner insists, to develop an orthodoxy which can perform the same function for the nationalist camp that Marxist ideology does for the Left. It is a great advantage to left-wing journalists, communists, and trade unions that they possess a common worldview. The nationalists, by contrast, lack a foundation which might otherwise solidify them into a bloc; instead, they are divided, only capable of uniting against a common "negative" target or enemy. Today, the Right needs a figure who can recreate what Lenin did for the Left, who can bring some systematic order to the clutter of nationalistic writings.

In his definition of "nationalism," Venner describes it as a return to ethnic community and a reaction against liberalism. It is the intention of nationalism, he says, to create new social relationships on a communitarian basis, as well as a political order based on a foundation of values and merit.[16] In his idea of Europe and his principles of action, Venner offers a universal solution to humanity's problems which have been caused by the Industrial Revolution. In the third segment of his book, he proposes a new definition of "nationalism." He begins with the "birth" of liberalism, dating its origin to the end of the 18th century. In his analysis, the success of liberalism stemmed from its status as a lever used by the high nobility and the bourgeoisie against the central government. In this struggle of the "big interests" against the power of the people (embodied by the French monarchy), he recognizes a recurring element in human history. While contemporary democracy represents a society that endorses "big interests" in their exploitation of the people, it is important to create a society that is based on the mass of the people in order to curb this dynamic. In contrast to democracies that have established rule by money and corruption, led chiefly by unscrupulous persons, the national revolution

---

16 Ibid., 38.

must remove these people and replace them with honourable actors willing to sacrifice themselves. In order to achieve this, the formation and selection of young men and their elites must take precedent in society. During training, it is critical to bend the inductees' self-will, increase their readiness for self-sacrifice, and foster their intellectual commitment to serious disciplines. Honourable character and a strict code form the foundation for a living order, which constantly renews itself over time, but remains unchanged in spirit. Consequently, the power of money would be replaced by the power of "believers and fighters." Venner concludes his positive critique with a vision of a nationalistic movement led by thousands of revolutionary cadres, one that casts the "conspiracists [and] careerists" to the periphery and banishes the nutcases, so as to offer a healthy medium for development and a high standard for membership.[17]

---

17   Ibid., 60.

Jean-François Thiriart
and the European Imperium

DOMINIQUE VENNER was not alone in his mission to bring about a reevaluation of the French Right and initiate a process of self-reflection. Jean-François Thiriart's (1922–1992) activism and writings strove for the same purpose. By his own account, the young Walloon suffered from an inferiority complex in his early days due to having been born in a small country. His family came from the triangle between the Netherlands (Maastricht), Belgium (Liège), and Germany (Aachen), the same geographico-historico-cultural context, that had fathered Charles Martel and Charlemagne, and it in turn nurtured Jean-François' Germanophile affections along with his romantic inclinations towards geopolitics.

Thiriart's political career is unique, as it led him from the Left to the Right: his political life began in the Unified Socialist Youth Guard (*Jeune Garde Socialiste Unifiée*) and the Socialist Anti-Fascist Union (*Socialiste Anti-Fasciste Union*). It was from there that he found his way to the national-revolutionary camp, to which he was introduced through the *Fichte-Bund* in Belgium. During his time among the radical Left, he began to develop an anti-bourgeois, pro-German orientation which led him, during the Second World War, to an organization known as the Friends of the Great German Reich (*Les Amis du Grand Reich Allemagne*), a Walloon group of the radical Left which supported collaboration with Germany. His collaboration with this group resulted in him being added to a proscription list by the Belgian *Résistance*. After the Allied liberation of Belgium, the national-revolutionary collaborator was sentenced under the reformed criminal code to one year's imprisonment; an interdiction was also imposed on his writings. The collapse of the Third Reich prompted him to reflect, which in turn caused him to reevaluate National Socialism and conclude that it was "stupid German nationalism and equally stupid anti-Slavic racism."[1]

Thiriart did not become active until 1960, when the decolonization of the Congo began. As was also the case with French Algeria, the Congo had been home to a community of Belgian settlers who had become embattled, and whose cause he wished to support. Yet, like Venner's attempt at retaining Algeria for France, Thiriart also failed in his advocacy for the preservation of the Belgian Congo. His commitment ultimately led him towards European nationalism: on March 4th, 1962, as a representative of the Movement of Civic Action (*Mouvement d'Action Civique*) in Venice under the leadership of Oswald Mosley, Thiriart met representatives of other political groups in Europe whose goal was the creation of a European national party that would fight against "American slavery." At the same time, they would fight for a united Europe "from Poland to Bulgaria via Hungary." However, as had happened with many previous European unification projects of the radical Right, this attempt also failed — the limited nationalism of its Italian and German participants spelled its end.

After the proposal to forge a Europe-wide movement out of various national movements had failed, Jean Thiriart turned to take a more revolutionary tack: in founding Young Europe (*Jeune Europe*) in 1963, he established a group that defined itself from its very onset as "pan-European." The project met with a positive response: in Belgium, the Netherlands, France, Switzerland, Austria, Germany, Italy, Spain, Portugal, and England, Thiriart managed to form tightly

---

1   Gene H. Hogberg, "Interview with Jean Thiriart, Part 2," trans. David Wainwright, *Counter Currents* (2010) [https://counter-currents.com/2010/09/interview-with-jean-thiriart-2/].

organized divisions under the sign of the Celtic Cross. But the number of members in Europe never exceeded 5,000, partially due to its ban in France, and partially because of their support for the OAS.

Thiriart formulated the theoretical tools for a united Europe in three works: first, in his *Manifesto for the European Nation* [*Le Manifeste à la Nation Européenne*] (1961), then expanded as *An Empire of 400 Million* [*Un empire de 400 millions d'hommes*] (1964),[2] and finally continued in *The Great Nation: A Unitarian Europe from Brest to Bucharest* [*La Grande Nation: l'Europe unitaire de Brest à Bucarest*] (1965). The aim of Thiriart's group was to unite Europe and develop it into a sovereign great power, for which the principle "neither Washington nor Moscow" applied. This "united, powerful, and communitarian Europe from Brest to Bucharest" was not to be a "federal Europe," but it was still meant to maintain its status as "a Europe of fatherlands." The argument for his model doubled as a rejection of "micro nationalisms," which he critiqued as the cause of the collapse of the new German Reich and the *Imperium Romanum.*

Thiriart clearly understood that there would be no Fourth German Reich. Instead, he posited a common European Imperium. The self-proclaimed "Jacobin of Great Europe" conceived of a centralistic European state structure, organized according to Leninist principles (organization of the masses, selection of its elites). More importantly, the group condemned "micro nationalisms that prevent the inhabitants of Europe from unification." The idea of a continentally organized European state followed from a purely geopolitical logic: so far, nation-states had been organized in terms of surface area, but, after the Second World War, nations could only be articulated within continental frameworks. Therefore, if Europe wished to survive against the United States, the Soviet Union, and China, it would be forced to become a unified nation. Only in a tactical alliance with China and the Arab states could a Europe of 400 million inhabitants

---

2   In English: Jean Thiriart, *Europe: An Empire of 400 Million*, trans. Alexander Jacob (London: Arktos, 2021).

reassert its sovereignty from its western to its eastern extremities. The rejection of an orientation towards Moscow or Washington also foreshadowed the economic objectives of the organization: the communitarianism conceived by Thiriart spurned both liberal capitalism and the planned economy, proposing instead a "European Socialism" with corporatist features. This was to be secured by a "Great Space [*Grossraum*] Economy" in an autarkic Europe, protected by tariffs. Likewise, he held the "circus of the United Nations" in contempt and advocated for a stronger collaboration with Latin America (with Spanish becoming Europe's *lingua franca*).

The then still embryonic "legal Europe" — the Europe of Strasbourg — came up against heavy resistance in its emphatic opposition to the "Europe of the Peoples" and the "European Nation." The organization developed a wide range of activities by the end of the 1960s, mainly in the journalistic field: alongside German and Italian magazines, the Francophone newspaper *La Nation Européenne* had been particularly successful in achieving a far-reaching synergy. Besides the French MP Francis Palmero, other contributors to its pages included the Syrian Ambassador in Brussels, Selim el-Yafi, the Iraqi ambassador in Paris, Nather Al-Omari, the Algerian Liberation Army officer and later Algerian minister, Chérif Belkacem, the head of the Việt Cộng mission in Algeria, Tran Hoai Nam, and the head of the Black Panther movement and Pan-Africanism, Stokely Carmichael; numerous other representatives of liberation movements from the third world and resistance movements from

Europe and America gave interviews for the magazine. In February 1969, it had even become possible to interview the former President of Argentina, Juan Peron, who was then living in exile in Madrid. Peron referred to Che Guevara and Fidel Castro as fighters for the liberation of Latin America who only sought refuge in the Soviet sphere of influence after the United States had threatened to destroy them. This outreach to the third world was also informed by practical considerations: the pan-European resistance movement depended on outside support. Like many on the radical Left in this period, Jean Thiriart was inspired by Latin America's struggle for liberation, and used it as a model for a projected armed wing of *Jeune Europe*. Moreover, in June 1966, at the initiative of Ceauşescu, Thiriart had a meeting with the Chinese Foreign Minister Zhou Enlai [周恩来] in Bucharest. Their discussion had been aimed at developing the Chinese strategy of a tri-continental resistance against the US, expanding it into a quad-continental bloc, with Europe acting as an "additional Vietnam." Like previous attempts in Algeria to construct a military-political organization, the talks with China failed.

Thiriart's logic for the talks was simple: as long as Germany, Italy, and Belgium remained satellites of the United States, one would be forced to train the future cadres of a revolutionary army in Africa; these cadres, after having completed their service in the Mediterranean and the Levant, would be capable of defeating the "American quislings. Thiriart was more successful in establishing contact with the Arabs. An activist of *Jeune Europe*, Roger Coudroy, had been killed in combat against the Israeli Army in his attempt to enter occupied Palestine with a squad under the command of Fatah. Coudroy was the first European to have sacrificed his life in the fight against Israel. During Thiriart's attempts to broaden this theater of action, he received initial support from Iraq and Syria, whose governments approved of his program. But, once the mass media and the Ba'athists had begun to clash, the Iraqi government (under Soviet pressure) was forced to withdraw its pledge of aid.

In 1969, Thiriart was resigned to defeat. Penniless and disappointed at the lack of any concrete support, he temporarily abandoned his political goals and returned to professional life. Shortly afterwards, *Jeune Europe* collapsed due to its leader's withdrawal. However, despite having retreated into private life, Thiriart never abandoned his theoretical deliberations; on the contrary, he developed them even further. In response to the Sino-American rapprochement led by Henry Kissinger in 1970s, Thiriart began to promote a Europe-Soviet alliance as a counterweight. Instead of "neither Washington nor Moscow," his new motto was "against Washington, with Moscow." As he said at the time, "If Moscow wishes to make Europe European, then I preach total collaboration. I will be the first to attach a Red Star to my cap. Soviet Europe — yes, without a doubt." Not even the Soviet collapse of 1991 could dissuade him from his dream of a united Great Europe, spanning from Dublin to

Vladivostok. The high point of his networking activity came in the form of a meeting held in Moscow in 1992. Along with Alain de Benoist and Robert Steuckers, he sought to organize a collaboration between the European Liberation Front (EFL) and the Eurasianist underground in Russia. It was at this meeting that the young Alexander Dugin encountered national-revolutionaries and Europeans belonging to the New Right who strove for liberation from American dominance.

Several months after his return from Moscow, Thiriart passed away at his Belgian home. Despite his geopolitical acumen, with which he was able to foresee a trade war between Europe and the United States as early as the 1980s, along with other friction in the transatlantic alliance, Thiriart remained, philosophically and politically, a child of modernity. Admittedly, he rejected both fascism and National Socialism, as well as liberalism, but he had never divorced himself from socialism (he had even planned a volume titled *The Transformation of Communism: Treaties on Enlightened Totalitarianism,* co-authored with José Cuadrado). The belligerent Walloon subscribed to a purely materialistic worldview, free from all transcendence, until the end of his life — a view that horrified the Italian Traditionalist Claudio Mutti, who was once inspired by Thiriart. Despite everything, Thiriart's vision of a world made up of continental blocs remains a dream which nonetheless continues to animate people amidst the current geopolitical upheaval.

The Birth of the New Right
out of the French Crisis

A MID THIS crisis of the French Right and the Gaullist republic, along with the economic boom and rapid modernization of France as it stared down a constant threat of annihilation during the Cold War, a new generation of men matured. Among them was a prominent thinker who has had a profound impact on European intellectual history. Born on December 11, 1943 in Saint-Symphorien (now part of Tours), the young Alain de Benoist had a "marginal" childhood, his parents hailing from the northern and northeastern peripheries of the country. While his mother traced her heritage from Norman and Breton peasantry, his father descended from Belgian aristocracy. Even though de Benoist had lived in Paris since the age of six, experiencing the vibrant life of the metropolis, he still spent plenty of time with his paternal grandmother in the countryside. From the cradle, young Alain had learned that *"noblesse oblige."*

Despite having met with a highly politicized climate towards the end of his school days, his engagement in politics only began after he had entered university in Paris. While there, he met the publicist Henry Coston, who inspired him to join the Federation of Nationalist Students (*Fédération des étudiants nationalistes*), of which he was a member from 1961 to 1965. De Benoist had not been a member of Dominique Venner's *Jeune Nation,* which had devastated the headquarters of the French Communist Party. Nevertheless, his time as a student was not limited to journalistic activities: it was marked by nightly activism and poster campaigns, brawls with left-wing students and demonstrations. Ultimately, he failed to graduate, not because he lacked the intellectual capacity or the necessary passion for writing, but because he refused to recognize the "French Regime."

When Dominique Venner was released from prison in 1962, de Benoist joined him at his new magazine *Europe-Action*, which was noteworthy for its merciless critique of the Old Right. The same strict line is reflected in their declaration of October 1963: "We understand that the struggle is to be led on political and not on military grounds, not by weapons but by ideas." With this statement, de Benoist had issued a clear rejection of "direct action" and revolutionary violence, as they only made sense under objectively revolutionary conditions. In all other instances, they contributed indirectly to "the established disOrder."[1] The new movement's non-violent *modus operandi* had been established, but the choice of means remained unclear. While, in the 1965 and 1966, the majority of members in the FEN urged the establishment of another right-wing party, which would fail as all previous attempts had, de Benoist proposed to establish an "Institute for Doctrinal Studies" that would consolidate the Right metapolitically, in accordance with contemporary standards. On July 2, 1967, Benoist finally left the FLN, together with Dominique Venner.[2] In the spring of 1968, prior to the leftist protests of the same year, the "New Right" (*Nouvelle Droite*) was born: on May 4–5, 1968, GRECE held its inaugural meeting.[3] Contrary to the rumors which had been circulating, Dominique Venner was not involved. But in what sense does this event qualify as the birth of New Right?

Originally, de Benoist referred to the novel school of thought as "New Culture," consciously striving to overcome the previous classifications of Left and Right. However, the French media resorted to their old methods and labelled his approach "right-wing." And so, out

---

1   Alain de Benoist, *Mein Leben. Wege eines Denkens* (Berlin: Junge Freiheit, 2014), 133.

2   Ibid., 128.

3   Ibid., 138.

of necessity, the enemy label was worn as a badge of honor. Even with the symbol of GRECE, de Benoist wished to walk untrodden paths: he had chosen a wickerwork motif from Irish-Gaelic art, which was too complicated for anyone to paint on city walls. This decision was meant to reflect years of activism in the national-revolutionary Right, which had distinguished itself not only by disseminating its own symbols, but also with its endless incantation of slogans, which people like de Benoist then repeated because they "corresponded to what 'we' were supposed to think."

The widespread allegation that the New Right was a reaction to the 1968 student movement and the New Left can be easily refuted in light of its earlier founding date (the GRECE founding conference took place in Lyon in early May 1968). The only similarity between the New Left and the New Right consists in the fact that both sides produced a new generation of intellectuals who strove to establish distance from the previous generation. While the New Left rejected Marxism-Leninism and Stalinism, the New Right directed its harshest critique against the "Old Right." As Alain de Benoist curtly articulated in his work *Cultural Revolution from the Right: Gramsci and the Nouvelle Droite*, "The Old Right is dead. It has earned its fate."[4] Whereas the Old Right had negative tendencies towards racism, colonialism, the cult of leadership, idolization of the past, Western chauvinism, and universalism, the New Right cast these attitudes into the dustbin of history and made a clean break. Likewise, they discarded the anti-intellectualism of the Old Right, which balked at theoretical discourses and self-criticism, making the repetition of previous failures inevitable. Another important difference between the New and Old Right is the former's rejection of narrow nationalism. By the era of globalization, such a position had become outdated; even the larger national states did not possess the resources necessary to assert their independence. Thus, the Jacobean idea was critiqued by

---

4   Alain de Benoist, *Kulturrevolution von rechts: Gramsci und die Nouvelle Droite* (Jungeuropa, 2017), 29.

the *Nouvelle Droite* firstly from a regional perspective, then from the perspective of the *Imperium*. They advocated for autonomy in regions belonging to larger states, while simultaneously rejecting micro-nationalisms. According to de Benoist, "micro-nationalism" bore the same defects as its "big brother."[5] They rejected colonialism, not only due to its inherent requirement of subjugation and domination, but primarily because of its expansionist nature. Colonialism demands that entire nations and ethnic groups be converted to the universalist Western European model, which by extension required that the colonized people's identity be uprooted. Instead of proclaiming itself a "universal" Western civilization, the *Nouvelle Droite* considers Europe to be its homeland, which, contrary to the "West," is not a fluid, progressive concept, but is rather an objective space with deep roots.[6]

However, while the tendency of the New Left to critique radical consumerism has been superseded by the pseudo-revolution of "desire" (de Benoist) and the airs of its egoistic, spoiled children, the New Right still fully retains its revolutionary vigour and a plasticity of thinking.[7] But this development should not be considered self-evident: not one year after GRECE's founding conference, only nine of the original thirty-six participants were still numbered in its ranks.[8] Alain de Benoist's decision to develop a think tank that did not strive to merely fulfill a determined political purpose (in the sense of a short-term political function) also contributed to its declining membership, as few shared his views. Even after 1969, there were newcomers and departures: for example, Yvan Blot, Jean-Yves Le Gallou, and Bernard Mazin left GRECE in 1973 with the aim of founding "a reservoir of ideas for the Right" in the *Club de l'Horloge*, only to ultimately merge with economic liberalism.[9]

---

5   Alain de Benoist, *Mein Leben*, 199–200.

6   Ibid., 201–203.

7   Ibid., 141.

8   Ibid., 139.

9   Ibid., 144–145.

Numerous fissures in the movement also resulted from de Benoist's initial vision of GRECE as being a combination of the Frankfurt School, *Action Française*, and a national institute for scholarship and activistic techniques. The group was aimed not at the political, but the metapolitical. The term "metapolitical" refers not to an alternative politics, but rather to that which precedes politics and makes it possible. To paraphrase Benoist, it is the "collective intellectual labor" that must carve out a path down which a politics may proceed. Such a "metaphysics of politics" (Joseph de Maistre, 1814) enable political changes and powerful political actions. The French Revolution became possible only by means of the spiritual revolution brought about by the Enlightenment; the October Revolution of 1917 materialized under Lenin only after Karl Marx had laid the ideological groundwork with his *Communist Manifesto*. "Cultural Power" lies at the origin of all political changes. Political change can only be implemented in society once it has taken place on a spiritual and moral level. The role of the intellectual and of cultural work consists in preparing for this change by providing the public with values, images, and themes that break with the ruling order and its own values. If one now ponders upon the importance of cultural power, newspaper offices, television series, it is because films and books are more important than electoral promises, commercials, or a televised rally of political parties.[10] But metapolitics is by no means in danger of becoming apolitical. On the contrary, the apolitical consists much more in wanting to engage in politics without having understood what politics is. The essence of metapolitics is found not on the level of political action, but on that of its intellectual preparation.[11] Against this background, the emergence of another GRECE emblem is illustrative: a head composed of two halves, one of them being that of the Greek philosopher Plato, and the other that of the Argentine Communist

---

10   Ibid., 145–146.

11   Ibid., 147.

and revolutionary leader Ernesto «Che» Guevara. This emblem combines the intellectual roots of Europe with the spirit of revolution.

De Benoist's idea of a "Gramscianism from the Right" came in the 1970s, after the founding of the *Nouvelle Droite* and the developmental phase which immediately followed. During this phase, he systematically dismantled and resolved numerous contradictions and issues inherited from the Old Right. One may mark the conclusion of this period with de Benoist's departure from the editorial staff of *Le Figaro Magazine* (a weekly supplement to what was then the most popular daily newspaper in France, *Le Figaro*). Thereafter, a period followed which lasted from the founding of *Krisis* magazine in 1988 until the early 1990s. During this time, the *Nouvelle Droite* discussed their positions and developed clear standpoints. With the end of this latter phase, we enter the period of the movement which persists to this day. It should be noted that the French *Nouvelle Droite* never limited itself to just one central organization, as was implied by the existence of GRECE. Instead, it achieved a wide impact through the dissemination of magazines, such as *Krisis, Nouvelle École*, and *Éléments,* as well as numerous other organs. During its systematic investigation of the intellectual landscape, the *Nouvelle Droite* benefited from favorable conditions, as a relatively open intellectual climate still prevailed in France during the 1970s. Thus, not only could the extreme Left and extreme Right disseminate their thought with relatively little obstruction, but the New Right had immediately attracted the attention of the influential post-war journalist Louis Pauwels, who wrote for *Le Figaro*.

Thanks to de Benoist's collection of essays *View from the Right*[12], which had won him a high profile, Pauwels offered him the opportunity to author his own weekly supplement for the daily newspaper

---

12 In English: Alain de Benoist, *View from the Right: A Critical Anthology of Contemporary Ideas, Volume I: Heritage and Foundations* (London: Arktos, 2017); idem, *View from the Right: A Critical Anthology of Contemporary Ideas, Volume II: Systems and Debates* (London: Arktos, 2018); idem, *View from the*

and eventually even coordinate his own column in *Figaro Magazine*. With a hand-picked editorial team, the men of the *Nouvelle Droite* succeeded in making their ideas known to a wider audience within France. Yet their readership reached further internationally, and travelled across half the globe, towards North and South America, Asia, and across Europe as far as Russia, which de Benoist visited a number of times at Alexander Dugin's invitation.[13] Admittedly, what emerged was not a "New Right Internationale," but a broader impact was achieved that resulted in the formation of a number of think tanks and intellectual circles, which met with more (the Italian *Nuova Destra* around Marco Tarchi) or less (the German *Neue Rechte* around the Thule-Seminar) success in disseminating their ideas.[14]

And so, the *Nouvelle Droite* had achieved its initial goals in the 1970s, having dodged the assaults of a press campaign against it and having increased in popularity. In the interim, Alain de Benoist also became acquainted with higher circles in politics. These acquaintances included entrepreneurs, but also financiers and large industrialists, as was the case during one conference in June of 1980. De Benoist was even offered a significant sum of money for renouncing the *Nouvelle Droite* and committing himself to liberalism, but he refused.[15] After the French media's strategy of public defamation had failed, the opposition resorted to more dishonorable methods.

From 1980 onwards, French banks and the advertising lobby finally began putting pressure on *Le Figaro Magazine*. These measures were accompanied by violent attacks from the extreme Left. In response, Louis Pauwels slowly began to dismiss his employees belonging to the *Nouvelle Droite*. The climate of free speech in France finally expired with the election of François Mitterrand to the presidency

---

Right: A Critical Anthology of Contemporary Ideas, Volume III: Controversies and Viewpoints (London: Arktos, 2019).

13   Alain de Benoist, *Mein Leben*, 154.

14   Ibid., 155.

15   Ibid., 164–165.

in 1981. The now established left-wing liberal hegemony pushed the ideas of the *Nouvelle Droite* to the fringes of society. But why was the New Right now subject to ostracization? De Benoist's book *Cultural Revolution from the Right* provides an answer.

Cultural Revolution: The Metapolitics of the New Right

THE FIRST edition of de Benoist's programmatic work in German, *Cultural Revolution from the Right*, was published in 1985. Over the course of the French New Right's gestation period, de Benoist had established numerous important principles which are encapsulated in this work's pages, establishing it as a reference work that is read to this day. The first chapter covers the contrast between the Old and the New Right. Beyond a reckoning with the Old Right ("she deserves her fate"), de Benoist proposes a new definition of the idea of the "Right." Whereas "Left" and "extreme Left" are clearly defined, the term "Right" was historically employed as a libelous epithet to be hurled at political opponents. De Benoist calls any position right-wing "that views the polymorphism of the world and its consequently relative inequalities, which are their necessary result, as good, and regards as evil the progressive unification of the world that has been realized over two thousand years by the discourse of egalitarian ideology and the actions it has inspired."[1]

In order to address the question of power anew, the Right must depart from its anti-intellectualism, which had lost it numerous important thinkers to the Left. Its civil adherence to the political parties as the sole form of political organization is also to be discarded against the backdrop of the Left's parliamentary successes. In order to become a relevant force in politics once more, as part of

---

1 Alain de Benoist, *Kulturrevolution von rechts: Gramsci und die Nouvelle Droite* (Jungeuropa, 2017), 30–31.

a positive-nihilistic turn, the Right must reinvent itself. In order for this to happen, it must discard and make a clean break with everything that has been associated with the Old Right. The key to freeing itself from this predicament was engaging with the question of cultural power. What de Benoist demands here, following the Italian communist Antonio Gramsci, is a conquest of the mind and, thus, a reflection on the metapolitical. De Benoist calls "metapolitical" that which Gramsci called "cultural power." In contrast to the Left, which remains aware of the importance of the metapolitical, the Right must first acknowledge the need to reacquire cultural power. Without publicly delegitimizing the political opponent and his ideas, such a thing is impossible to achieve. This also means that the New Right must occupy itself once again with current ideas, so that it can offer alternatives to liberal society, a mission which the Old Right had failed. This is of the greatest necessity because, with the steady dissolution of the liberal "order," the need for new ideas grows stronger. The theorists' vengeance in history, de Benoist posits, is that revolution is only the political sanctioning of a change that has already taken place in the mind. There would have been no Lenin without Karl Marx, no American Revolution without the Enlightenment and the idea of human rights. To save Europe, simple reforms are insufficient. What is needed is a cultural revolution from the Right.

The second major topic de Benoist addresses in the book is the issue of racism. In the form of an interview, he explains how we face various forms of racism today. One of them is the classic xenophobic racism, which always looks to blame the other, condemning the other because of their otherness and reducing them to a scapegoat. On the other hand, there is a so-called anti-racism which speaks constantly about "people," "human rights," and all-embracing philanthropy, but can think of no solution to the conflicts persisting between the various races. According to de Benoist, problems, if they exist, have to be clearly identified; otherwise, no solution is possible. This cannot be realized by establishing a racial hierarchy. Moreover, there is an inherent genius in every race which refutes the reduction of humans to a zoological category, for humans are bearers of history, culture, and fate.[2] The peoples that embody exactly these distinct ethnic characteristics would see their identity threatened not only by racism, but also by individualism. De Benoist ultimately condemns not only racism, but also anti-racism, since the latter leads likewise to the levelling of identities in the name of progress, universalism, and egalitarianism.[3] De Benoist considers the notion of a "white solidarity" to be an absurdity, invoking the Cold War rivalry between the white powers of the United States and the Soviet Union which, in turn, had completely different interests than those of Europe. Alternatively, Europe must address the young nations of the Third World, which are the only ones in the position "to restore the necessary plurality to power dynamics in the world."[4]

De Benoist rejects immigration on the grounds that it serves only the interests of the large corporations and debilitates the innovative strength of one's own society. Furthermore, he argues that immigration leads to a loss of identity among both the natives and immigrants, generating ethnic tensions. In this context, he also rejects the integration and assimilation of immigrants, as this leads to the destruction of their own identity.[5] To the idea of Western universalism, discrimination (in the sense of unequal treatment), and the geopolitical hegemony of the West, de Benoist counterposes non-discrimination, mutual decolonization (which concerns all forms of colonization, including strategic, economic, and cultural), and nations' right to self-determination. Against the free movement of people all over the world in the service of the free market, de Benoist ultimately calls upon a simple and logical principle: the right of nations to be

---

2   Ibid., 85.

3   Ibid., 87.

4   Ibid., 96.

5   Ibid., 99–101.

themselves and to reach their full development, posed in opposition to all forms of racism and universalism. This, finally, leads to his concept of ethnopluralism.

In a subsequent chapter, de Benoist discusses the importance of rootedness in soil. Just as every animal calls a certain territory its own, humans are rooted in the soil which they cultivate and on which they live. The tragedy of nationalism now lies in that it does not recognize this fundamental principle.[6] Therefore, according to de Benoist, it is the task of the New Right to reflect on this rootedness in the homeland in order not to drift into liberalism (more specifically, neoliberalism). Movements have merged which have claimed to be in search of their identity, but which were diverted into intellectual currents completely foreign to them. They have alienated themselves from their own identity and region by adhering to egalitarian and levelling ideologies, whose presuppositions fundamentally oppose the concepts of diversity and authenticity. According to de Benoist, this is appalling and unacceptable.[7] Thus, the spiritual father of the *Nouvelle Droite* does not promote any form of collectivism; rather, he emphasizes the importance of community which, in his eyes, is embattled on two fronts in modernity. This two-sided menace is is known by the terms "individualism" and "collectivism." According to Benoist, the wealth of humanity lies in the individual's discovering

---

6   When it comes to de Benoist's critique of nationalism, we always have to keep in mind that he formulates it from a French perspective. Both French/Jacobin nationalism and German nationalism defined themselves by fighting against the regional identities, dialects, customs, etc. which already existed before French/German nationalism came into being as artificial constructs. De Benoist critiques nationalism precisely because it attacks such rooted identities. In France, for example, French nationalism took the identity of Île-de-France, the capital region, and tried to turn every Frenchman, whether one was originally from Bretagne or Aquitaine, into a Parisian. The same goes for Prussian identity in Germany, which tried to standardize/uniformize all the Bavarians, Saxonians, etc., into Prussians.

7   de Benoist, *Kulturrevolution von rechts*, 114.

of personality within community. The wealth of Europe, in turn, is based on the personality of the regions within the culture of the civilization from which they originate. Of critical importance here is the notion that these personalities should coexist in an overarching interrelationship. The plurality is, therefore, also necessarily dialectical. A community will always be simultaneously threatened by individualism and collectivism, never by a modern identity construction alone. Only when European nations respect the differences that exist on the continent, on the individual and ethnic levels, can Europe's freedom be secured.

In the fifth chapter, de Benoist focuses on an important question concerning the future of Europe: the continent's future elite. Tracing the emergence of the bourgeoisie, beginning from the Middle Ages, he demonstrates that it was precisely bourgeois-liberal society that pursued the establishment of functionary elites. He argues that Europe does not require new functionaries, who have only been good for cultivating servility to the regime and criminality towards the populace. Instead, he says that what our continent requires is an elite of character, a new aristocracy. Citing Nietzsche's dictum that "spirit does not ennoble; rather, something is needed that ennobles spirit," de Benoist does not call for a "new elite" *per se*, but rather states the need for a new standard for character and backbone. A character such as this would naturally lead to the organic emergence of a new aristocracy. Creating this new aristocracy means instructing a group that is capable of educating the people and reconciling class antagonisms that have arisen with the ascent of the bourgeoisie. As a result of the ascent of the bourgeoisie, all aspects of human life have been reduced to their economic utility, argues de Benoist. Moreover, this has generated a creeping process whereby the economy has gradually come to replace politics. In light of the spiritual impoverishment that has been induced by materialism, the need for a new aristocracy has become even more acute. There has been a direct proportional relationship between the rapid growth of material wealth and rising levels of intellectual poverty. Refusal to accept responsibility, either individually or collectively, has become a mass phenomenon. This tendency is conditioned by the mass media, which have reinforced these attitudes and inculcated a lack of will in consumers. Various means have been employed to achieve this state of affairs, including the subversive lionization of anti-heroes in films and television.

In his passionate address to Germans, de Benoist entreats them to endow themselves with a spiritual form as a people. In this regard, he explicitly emphasizes the German Conservative Revolution, alluding to the New Right's admiration for this philosophical and spiritual phenomenon. In particular, he points out the distinct German trait of striving for excellence in every field. Yet, his endorsement is not uncritical: as he says, this German characteristic is capable of both great achievements and great crimes. This is not least because the German soul has no nature at its fundament, and must instead fashion one for itself, lest it should perish. Alain de Benoist notes with regret that the Germans have now found themselves at precisely such a decisive precipice. If the German spirit is in its own Elysium, then it will find a way to clamber up to it. In another chapter, he calls for the Germans to rediscover their identity and to distance themselves from extremism. For, without Germany, Europe cannot become independent.

The last two chapters of the book engage with the ideology of liberalism. De Benoist first addresses the question of totalitarianism, inquiring into its essence and bases. His conclusion is that liberalism, too, has its form of totalitarianism. Furthermore, he establishes that the underlying roots of totalitarianism are to be found in the pursuit of total equality and, by extension, egalitarianism. It turns out that the West is anything but immune to totalitarianism; on the contrary, it is extremely vulnerable to it. Since liberal democracy runs the risk of collapsing into a totalitarian democracy at any time, being latently connected to it, liberal democracy can hardly serve as protection against totalitarianism. Only by breaking out of the ideology of egalitarianism and materialism, to which the world fell victim in the 18th century, can totalitarianism be effectively countered, since this represents the common breeding ground for both liberal and totalitarian democracy.

At the dawn of the Cold War, two children of modernity — liberalism and communism — were in conflict. The question as to which of the two is more dangerous is answered in the book's final chapter, "The Main Enemy." In this section, de Benoist investigates the inherent familial ties between liberalism and communism. Liberalism, it turns out, has been the unequivocal archfiend of Europe. Hence the necessity for the New Right to articulate theoretical alternatives. This work, which is still ongoing, was urgent at that time, given that the fruits of the Cold War had grown from the seeds of 19th-century Marxism. It had only taken seventy years for the Bolshevik Revolution to occur after the publication of the *Communist Manifesto*. History knows no shortcuts, and those who attempt to find one inevitably fail. The New Right, however, should do everything humanly possible to avoid choosing between East and West, communism and liberalism. Indeed, if the choice were limited only to these options, it would not be a choice at all. Under the pressure of such a compulsory decision, one must take a position. And so, the New Right holds that every dictatorship is contemptible, yet decadence is more contemptible still. While dictatorship can destroy the individual at a moment's notice, decadence destroys the chances of survival of an entire nation.

Following in the tradition of Charles de Gaulle, Alain de Benoist makes the point that, despite communism's unprecedented brutality, liberalism is more destructive because of its corrosive effect on the souls of nations. He resolutely oppose those who believe that the struggle against liberalism favors communism. Declaring liberalism the archfiend under the above conditions does not mean becoming the right-hand of Moscow. Quite to the contrary, the only effective way to combat communism is to combat what has created it. When liberals denounce the "communist danger," they only reveal their own ineptitude in averting this danger. With their ideas, actions, and omissions, they only evoke the thing for which they are responsible. Because of its inherent anti-egalitarianism, the New Right is not only an opponent of communism, but also an enemy of liberalism.

Ethnopluralism and Differential Anti-Racism: Love for One's Own and the Multiplicity of Peoples

I F THERE is one representative of the New Right who has enjoyed comparatively little recognition, it is Henning Eichberg (1942–2017). The young graduate in sports science encountered GRECE and Alain de Benoist in the late 1960s and distinguished himself mainly through one concept: *ethnopluralism*. Composed of the words "ethnicity" and "pluralism," it refers to the multiplicity of peoples, the self-determination and development of every people on their ancestral territory. But what are the dimensions of this concept and how did its development lead to Alain de Benoist's own concept of "differential anti-racism?" In order to make sense of this, we must first sketch Henning Eichberg's journey through life, leading up to the beginnings of the German New Right.

Eichberg worked not only as the German correspondent for the New Right magazine *Nouvelle École*, but he also drafted a policy statement for the breakaway National-Democratic Party of Germany [*Nationaldemokratische Partei Deutschlands, NDP*], "Action New Right," in which he introduced his concept of *ethnopluralism*. He debuted the concept in a 1980 special issue of *Wir selbst* (We Ourselves). The term is not specifically mentioned in any other context than that provided by Eichberg. But what does ethnopluralism currently represent?

Ralf Laubenheimer begins his article "Nationalism as an Emancipatory Movement" by postulating that humans, as social beings, are dominated by a fundamental need for togetherness, expressed inwardly through "integration" and outwardly through "demarcation."[1] From the awareness of collective togetherness arises a will for self-affirmation, and this ultimately leads to demands for self-determination, self-government, and self-rule.[2] Thus, he exhibits the contrast between nationalism (which is understood here in terms of ethnocentrism) and chauvinism. This stipulates that there is no logic necessarily leading from a people's sense of unity and their will to self-determination to their expansion of power over other peoples. Rather, it is only the logic of capitalism and imperialism which leads to the compulsion to conquer new markets and oppress other peoples. Instead, he believes that it makes sense to limit oneself to the nation's regulatory framework. One's right to national identity and a state can only exist if all other peoples can enjoy the same right. Tolerance and respect for the otherness of other peoples should be a fundamental principle of nationalism.[3]

In an interview with *Wir selbst*, Henning Eichberg explains another important aspect of ethnopluralism, namely its critique of individualism. Germany, as an occupied territory, is confronted by economic, political, and cultural imperialism. The occupation is tangible in all spheres of everyday life. This system, which is destroying the German people, confronts us in two forms — that of military occupation and that of the multinational corporations. The general alienation created by industrial society must be countered with a new identity. The individual cannot be the only frame of reference, because the logic of the absolute individual leads to death by overdose. Rather, the new identity must be a collective one, possessing both a regional and a national dimension.[4] Another important aspect of ethnoplu-

---

1   *Wir selbst* 3 (1980), 4.

2   Ibid., 5.

3   Ibid., 6.

4   Ibid., 10.

ralism is its attitude toward borders. One must live with them without being restricted by them, Eichberg holds. It is possible to be a man, a woman, or perhaps a hermaphrodite, but one cannot be qualitatively all three at once. Man is limited in his existence and must be one thing or another, in one place or in another. In such limitations lies his richness. Without the other, there would be no recognition of oneself and, without the nation, there could be no internationalism; consequently, there could be no dialogue between nations.[5]

Shortly afterwards, having been labeled a "right-winger" and suffering academic ostracization, Eichberg fled his homeland for Denmark. Once there, he joined the Socialist People's Party [*Socialistisk Folkeparti*] and made a political move to the Left. In the successor magazine of *Wir selbst*, *Volkslust* (The People's Desire) — whose pages were host to other successful authors such as Ellen Kositza — Eichberg continued to develop his thesis that individualization is a threat to the people and therefore to the diversity of peoples. Attempts are increasingly made to replace the word "people" with "population." This process involves more than just cosmetic linguistics, since it renders "we" as the subject of social action invisible and replaces it with "that" as a category of administrative control. On another axis, an attempt is made to replace the "*demos*" or the "people" of democracy with the individual "citizen," who is not integrated into a larger collective subject of political action, but stands alone in isolation. This neoliberal individualization strategy leads to the destruction of society, the term "fellow citizenship" [*Mitbürgerismus*] having been turned against the premodern and anti-bourgeois popular terms. It should give us pause that the modern term "people" (*Volk*) emerged contemporaneously with the institution of representative, parliamentarian democracy. The concept of democracy also presupposes a notion of "peoplehood" or "*ethnos*." Hence, the theory of democracy has always been subordinated to the theory of the state,

---

5   Ibid., 9.

for which any formulation of the actual "people" is irrelevant. But if "the people" are removed from the definition of democracy, all that remains of the idea of "rule of the people" is the notion of "rule."[6]

In the *Manifesto for a European Renaissance* (understood by some as a declaration of war on Huntington's thesis of the "clash of civilizations"), Alain de Benoist further brings into relief the connection between people and democracy.[7] Liberalism is the opposite of democracy, because it is inherently destructive to the identity and freedom of peoples. Nowadays, we require more direct democracy, but such a democracy can only be practiced at the grassroots level, within communities that have specific *nomoi*, or shared values. This implies extensive autonomy at all levels, a federative restructuring of society, and a systematic application of the subsidiarity principle, according to which each level should assign to the next only those problems which it cannot solve on its own. Since it is based on individualism, liberalism tends to break down all types of relations that transcend the individual. Since optimal market operations presuppose no hinderances to the free movement of people and goods, there should be no limitations of any kind, to include those naturally imposed by organic social structures; and so, these structures must necessarily be dissolved. It is therefore unsurprising that the rise of liberal individualism initially led to a gradual dissolution of holistic societies and organic lifestyles. The next step is the dissolution of social ties and, ultimately, social *anomie*, a war of all against all in which individuals become increasingly alien and hostile to one another, at which point a conclusive dehumanization sets in.

For de Benoist, the decisive principle to be set in opposition to the "individual" is that of collective identity. According to him, this

---

6   Henning Eichberg, "Volk wer, wo, was oder warum nicht? Arbeitsthesen zu einer humanwissenschaftlichen Volkstheorie," *Volkslust* 1 (2004).

7   Alain de Benoist and Charles Champetier, *Manifesto for a European Renaissance* (London: Arktos, 2012); German edition: Alain de Benoist, *Aufstand der Kulturen: Europäisches Manifest für das 21. Jahrhundert* (Junge Freiheit, 2019).

identity is not static, but always changing. One ought not merely refer to established historical iterations of identity, using these as a safe haven which would insulate one from the ravages of the present. Rather, this understanding of identity would allow one to grasp that which remains stable in the interplay of differences; this thing does not stay the same, but inheres as a special way of changing, without ever departing from the self. According to de Benoist, the loss of European identity is the result not of immigration, but of the technical, economic unification of the world, whose main agent is a supranational liberal imperialism with America as its center. The French and Germans would lose their identity with or without immigration as a result of their own negligence, de Benoist asserts. Foreigners would ultimately serve only as good scapegoats. Both racism and anti-racism are universalistic, since the former absolutizes the biological component, while the latter denies biology's very existence; even anti-racism is racist, since it denies ethnic groups the right to exist. De Benoist himself advocates a differentialist anti-racism which, in contrast to universalist anti-racism, would recognize the diversity of peoples and their differences. Unlike racism, this differential model would not view the biology of these distinct peoples as absolute and unchanging. This is the position of the New Right.

The Therapeutic State

I n *Cultural Revolution from the Right,* Alain de Benoist explains that liberalism can easily tip over into a totalitarian democracy. But how exactly does such liberal totalitarianism manifest itself in the 21st century? The American historian Paul Edward Gottfried investigates this issue. Born in 1941, the son of Austrian Jewish emigres who had fled from National Socialist Germany, he studied history at Yale University in the 1960s. There, he made the acquaintance of figures involved in the Frankfurt School (*Frankfurter Schule für Sozialforschung*), including one of its leading exponents, the neo-Marxist Herbert Marcuse. Similar to the representatives of the New Right in Europe, Paul Gottfried developed an early predilection for the ideas which had flowed from the Conservative Revolution, with Carl Schmitt and Martin Heidegger drawing the historian's particular interest.[1] In addition, he harbored a deep admiration for the intellectual history of German Romanticism. As part of his engagement with liberal ideology, Gottfried pursued a question which had been initially raised by Eric Voegelin: to what extent has modern thinking been affected by distorted elements of Christianity following the Enlightenment?

The emergence of the paleoconservatives — which may be described as the American counterpart to the New Right — occurred

---

1   To take one example of his enthusiasm for the philosophy of the Conservative Revolution, Gottfried wrote the preface to the 2018 English edition of the standard reference work on the movement by Armin Mohler and Karlheinz Weissman: *The Conservative Revolution in Germany, 1918–1932* (Radix, 2018).

through a series of detours. As a member of the Republican Party, Paul Gottfried supported Ronald Reagan's candidacy in the 1980s, attracted as he was by the future president's patriotic rhetoric; this endorsement prefigured that of certain right-wing elements in America who would later support Donald Trump in 2016. In retrospect, Gottfried bitterly regretted his decision in light of Reagan's neoconservative policies. He documented this disappointment as a critique of neoconservatism in his book *The Search for Historical Meaning* (1987).[2]

From this point on, his thinking was marked by a deep skepticism towards Neo-conservatism. Henceforth, he would characterize it as follows: for the fake Right, in its opposition to any genuinely counterrevolutionary force, the egalitarian project takes on an even more aggressive form within the scope of the "global American democratic mission." Suddenly, it becomes the duty of the American superpower and its "allies" to export women's rights and other blessings of the current global regime to societies that are regarded as less developed. This mission is heralded either in the name of "American values" or of modernizing the world, which the United States is obligated to do for humanitarian reasons, or because "liberal democracy" is nowhere secure as long as it is not fully implemented on a worldwide scale.[3] From that moment onwards, Gottfried positioned himself as a critic of neoconservatism and human rights, and opposed the idea of the United States of America as a "propositional nation," which denies the original character of the United States as a European colony.

Gottfried's critique turned not only against the neoconservatives, but also against the entire American Right, which he perceived as having been ideologically derailed. Adhering to the tradition of the Conservative Revolution in its American inflection, and developing its critique of the liberal administrative state, Gottfried wrote

---

2   Paul Gottfried, *The Search for Historical Meaning: Hegel and the Postwar American Right* (Northern Illinois University Press, 1987).

3   Paul Gottfried, *War and Democracy* (London: Arktos, 2012), 9.

a three-part series of books: *After Liberalism: Mass Democracy in the Managerial State* (2001), *Multiculturalism and the Politics of Guilt: Toward a Secular Theocracy* (2002), and *The Strange Death of Marxism: The European Left in the New Millennium* (2005). Instead of supporting the contemporary liberal American Right, he founded the school of paleoconservatism, whose prefix "paleo-" referrs to an about-face from the platform of the "neoconservatives" in favor of restoring the traditions of the old American Right. Moreover, it implies a commitment to the European heritage of the United States, as well as a fundamental critique of modernity from within the framework of traditional thinking. Other representatives of this school of thought include the author and politician Pat Buchanan and Samuel T. Francis. Talented in the coining of terms, Gottfried also devised the now well-known concept of the "Alternative Right" and promoted its current figurehead Richard Spencer, who managed to popularize his mentor's coinage while nonetheless removing himself from its associated ideology. The latter's modernist "race realism," fixated on the category of biological race, stands in stark contrast to Gottfried's desire for European-Americans to return to their European heritage.

Central to Gottfried's thought is the concept of "political religion," which emerged from his analysis of the way in which secular ideologies in the modern era have tended to substitute themselves for religious beliefs. According to Gottfried, the chiliastic expectations and presentism underpinning modern politics are the product of an obsessive egalitarianism. The main features of the current *Zeitgeist* include a denial of genetic differences between groups, an enthusiasm for "lifestyles" that were once classified as perverse (now associated with Mircea Eliade's concept of the "righteous sufferer"), and the destruction of gender roles as something oppressive and hierarchical belonging to the "dustbin of history." This stance corrupts historical interpretation and makes it virtually impossible to observe earlier ages without evaluating them from the perspective of the current hierarchy of victimhood. Any deviation in the past from this imposed model of preferred victims and the sensitivities required to interact with them is taken as evidence of an inexcusable reactionary attitude.

In liberal ideology Gottfried recognizes above all a pathological mania for equality. It is the constant propaganda of those who have now been elevated as the new protagonists of a therapeutic politics of guilt. The latter, be they homosexuals, ethnic minorities, or other marginalized groups, have stylized themselves as "victims of the majority." According to Mircea Eliade, this is the result of a distorted Christianity, from which liberalism has derived the idea of the "righteous sufferer." According to the sociologist Jacques Ellul and the cultural historian René Girard, this turn lent the ideology of Progress a religious attraction by integrating reinterpreted Christian ideas into the therapeutic politics of the present. The updated notion of the "righteous sufferer" refers at one moment to the Third World and at another moment to those who have been victimized because of their gender-non-conformity — all on demand to suit a given situation.[4] The liberal state, which considers its primary task to be the administration of the population, thus becomes a therapeutic state, whose task now consists in enforcing positive discrimination measures against a majority population that is viewed as racist/fascist or homophobic *vis-à-vis* their alleged victims. The religious motifs acquired in the process serve solely to advance the therapeutic form of rule by discrediting moral resistance.[5]

Have homophobic remarks been uttered in school? Then social workers are sent to the schools to promote homosexual lifestyles there, as has occurred in New York and other states, to provide positive support to those who have been discriminated against. Ultimately, such events serve as justification for "positive discrimination," which is to say an equal or improved status for minorities. But should one defend himself against this new status-quo, he is silenced

---

4   Paul Gottfried, *Mulitikulturalismus und die Politik der Schuld* (Ares Verlag, 2004), 194.

5   Ibid., 195.

by anti-discrimination laws under accusations of hate speech. The majority of people, who are neither homosexual, pedophilic, nor abnormal in any way, are treated as an aberrant element by such policies, classed together with the mentally ill. Whoever stands up against the egalitarian demands of liberalism and its intentional dissolution of collective identities runs the risk of being branded a "racist," "fascist" and "sexist," and eventually condemned to public execution (as the ultimate logical conclusion of the ideology). As a result of positive discrimination, not only are minorities of all categories politically strengthened and mobilized, but the majority is also demobilized and gradually deprived of their rights.

In the context of the politics of guilt, the collective identity of the autochthonous people is demonized and presented as contemptible. This is done by cutting off the historical roots of the people and painting them as contemptible *vis-à-vis* the progressive racism directed against the past; thus, the majority is reduced to something singularly negative. In the cases of Great Britain and France, the colonial period must be castigated; in the case of German history, it is National Socialism that is used as a moral cudgel. Nations bereft of either a fascist or colonialist past are subjected to an inquisition for their ubiquitous "everyday racism," Sweden being a case-in-point. The consequence of this policy of guilt is a severe identity crisis which, if perpetuated over the course of several decades, can cause a people to lose their will to exist. The result is a soft totalitarianism that arises primarily from the anti-democratic character of the politics of guilt. Homosexual rights, feminism, multicultural behaviorism, and liberal immigration ideology are the foundations of a politics imposed from above, instead of being elected from below.

By mobilizing minorities against the majority while demobilizing and disenfranchising the people, a never-ending conflict is precipitated which can flare up at any time. Paul Gottfried quotes Stanley Renshon in this context, who dares to claim that a fundamental conflict has arisen between people of different racial, ethnic, and cultural origins who perceive themselves to be disadvantaged and those who regard these people as culturally privileged.[6] The resulting conflict knows neither a temporal nor a spatial limitation. So, while the people are increasingly living in a nightmare of constant terror and civil-war-like conditions, the therapeutic state sees a wonderful opportunity to further expand its powers of control, repression, and therapy. From a sociological perspective, this leads to the self-abolition of the modern nation-state through the destruction of the very idea of the nation. What remains are solitary, bourgeois, individual subjects who have been deprived of any protective community, and have therefore been lumped into a global society that ultimately strives for the establishment of a world state as the final goal of liberalism. From this point of view, it would be wrong to say that this process of destruction is being carried out for its own sake. Rather, the authorities behind the therapeutic state, be they social workers, university professors, human rights activists, or spokesmen from various minorities, drive the idea that they are fighting for a just goal in their commitment to the utopia of a global liberal state which propagates human rights. In their imagination, they represent the absolute moral good, just as the Jacobins thought of themselves during the *Grande Terreur*, the Communists did during their various "purges," and the National Socialists did during their genocides and wars of extermination.

For Paul Gottfried, given the current state of Western nations, a very pessimistic picture emerges. In his view, the damage caused by the politics of guilt is already irreparable. It is difficult for him to imagine how the atrophied social institutions of the West, beginning with the weakened family, might still be revived so as to create a social system that could take the place of the statutory social-security state. In this sense, he considers the liberal system to be extremely stable, despite its destructive tendencies. According to Gottfried, it can be clearly ascertained that the current liberal-Protestant

---

6   Ibid., 203.

worldview is in no way in danger of being superseded.[7] The administrators of this worldview — the media as well as the academic priesthood — work out of ideological obstinacy and the prospect of short-term gains for those outstretched hands parasitically benefitting from multiculturalism. It is only a matter of time, Gottfried warns, before Chicano racists, Third World patriarchs, and Mexican irredentists overwhelm the demographics of the United States and capture the government.

---

7   Ibid., 197.

Renaud Camus and the Great Replacement

THE TERM "Great Replacement" is appearing with increasing regularity not only in the slogans and fliers of mass demonstrations, but also in the alarmist reports on right-wing extremism put out by the German intelligence service (the Federal Office for the Protection of the Constitution) as well as in many utterances of Europe's New Right organizations themselves. But what does this term actually mean, and who contributed to its popularization? The man who has brought the "Great Replacement" into the public consciousness is Renaud Camus, born in 1946 in Chamalières, Puy-de-Dôme, in central France. Compared to other representatives of the New Right, Camus did not decide to oppose liberalism until later in his life. As a homosexual, he fought for the expansion of gay rights in France. An admirer of British culture (particularly that of Scotland), he penned numerous famous travel books on the subject. His cosmopolitan life took him from New York to Rome, where he made acquaintances with the international art scene and befriended Andy Warhol, among others.

Only after he realized the taboo of being a patriot did his patriotism become the dominant expression of his political will. Camus could not comprehend how the citizens of European countries were not in unbearable agony over such a dirty, stupid, despicable death of their societies, especially in the French context.[1] The impending fall of France, and Europe more broadly, provoked Camus to carry

---

1 Martin Lichtmesz, "Renaud Camus und der Große Austausch" in Renaud Camus, *Revolte gegen den Großen Austausch* (Antaios, 2015), 12.

out a philosophical analysis of the predicament. To counteract this development, he launched an initiative called "No to the replacement of people and civilization" (*Non au changement de peuple et de civilization*). Remaining faithful to his essence as a man of letters, Camus repeatedly coined new terms and popularized them. His biggest success so far is the term "The Great Replacement" (*Le Grand Remplacement*), which has now become a household idea. This term refers both to Europeans' lack of will to procreate and ensure their future, and to immigrants' willingness to occupy this vacuum and replace their childless rivals. The Global South that has come to stake its claim in Europe. The ultimate outcome of the Great Replacement will not be a new Europe with "new Europeans," but rather a total eradication of Europe as such.

Who is behind the Great Replacement? According to Camus, this is not some fateful, extra-human process, but a plan designed and executed by the corrupt liberal elite which, in its spirit of capitalism, multiculturalism, and pathological hatred for the native population, reduces immigration to a question of labor supply. This is motivated by the logic of the "end of history," which reduces the whole of life to economic considerations, such as gross national product and balance of trade. Still, the Great Replacement is only possible following the prior destruction of the autochthonous culture, along with the total economization of all areas of life that sees Europeans robbed of their heritage and reduced to mere atomized individuals.[2] In turn, this large-scale dismantling of culture is based on the idea that all people are interchangeable individuals.[3] According to Camus, this is a product of liberal ideology and merely serves the advance of globalization, the result of which is the ongoing dissolution of all national, ethnic, and cultural contours. Having been deterritorialized from birth, the liberal subject can be dislocated at will, manipulated, and employed

---

2   Camus, *Revolte gegen den Großen Austausch*, 60.

3   Ibid., 60–61.

as a cog in the machinery of international finance and the global circulation of goods.

On the other hand, Renaud Camus regards the current mass immigration to Europe as a kind of counter-colonization, in which context the peoples of the South aspire to enjoy Western prosperity. At the same time, Camus is of the opinion that this plan cannot function in the long-term. This is because the immigrants do not understand that the prosperity which has made their targeted societies so attractive is the result of a long asceticism that was only made possible by a generally accepted social contract. But immigrants tend to bring their own identities and mentalities with them when escaping their home countries and arriving in the country hosting them. In the host nation, they waste no time on recreating the conditions which had made their home countries so unbearable. People tend not to notice the paradox of this behavior.[4] This behavior also includes "transgressions" (*nocences*), a term which Camus uses to describe the almost daily rapes, murders, and terrorist attacks carried out by immigrants. In the eyes of the French writer, this is a form of "irregular warfare" (IW), designed to clear space for the settlers by displacing the autochthonous Europeans — a process colloquially called "white flight." Thus, counter-colonization also leads to land-grabbing by the new overlords. According to Camus, the complicity of Western media in this process consists in depriving every man and women of trust in their own sensory perception.[5] Imposed language regulations stigmatize words such as "folk" and all other terms expressive of a collective identity. Instead of addressing the actual problem (the Great Replacement), the media uses shame to foreclose on any prospect of public debate. In reality, neither the violence nor the threats to domestic security are as devastating a development as the state censorship apparatus. Renaud Camus argues that the real problem is

---

4   Ibid., 71.

5   Ibid., 95.

mass immigration, the large-scale replacement of native peoples in European countries ultimately leading to the dissolution of European civilization, in the meanwhile taking on the form of compelled coexistence between the native civilization and the immigrant civilization, which Camus sees as a battle of conquest for resources and living space.[6]

But how can one stop this development? According to Camus, one must first stop the swing of the pendulum from the direction of renewed colonization and, secondly, steer it in the opposite direction. He hopes that this new war of independence can be fought primarily by means of law, contracts and contract terminations, politics, and police — that is, by will and perseverance instead of blood and tears.[7] Immigration must be put to an immediate end and the repatriation of immigrants set in motion. Immigrants without citizenship should be deprived of the hope of being granted citizenship unless they have made special contributions to their adoptive country. Furthermore, the legal differences between immigrants and locals should be more clearly articulated. With regards to the welfare state, Camus proposes depriving immigrants of all incentives and redesigning social policy from the ground up. Besides the classic right-wing demands like the expulsion of all criminal foreigners and those who disparage France and its people, he pleads for the same identitarian policy as that of the French Canadians in Québec. This means defining what constitutes one's own country and what does not, as well as refusing to conform to the customs of immigrants.[8] It is also noteworthy that Camus points out that France has never offered immigrants a culture which they were capable of adopting; instead, all it has made available to them is an open void. Accordingly, at the beginning of the struggle against the Great Replacement, there must be a reaffirmation of one's

---

6   Ibid., 105.

7   Ibid., 131.

8   Ibid., 133.

own culture, formulated within a pan-European framework, since all European peoples are subject to the same bondage. After all, Europe cannot liberate itself without the aid of the French, and the French are equally powerless without all of Europe behind it.[9]

9   Ibid., 135–136.

The Populist Moment: The Hour of the People's Uprising against Liberalism?

I N H I S book *The Populist Moment: The End of Left vs. Right* (*Le moment populiste. Droite-gauche, c'est fini!*), published in 2017, Alain de Benoist addresses the phenomenon of populism. By analyzing the meaning of the concept, he dispels several aspects of the confusion surrounding the term. First, he explores the bases of "populism" from the elite perspective: in the eyes of society's brahmins, populism is first and foremost an illusion, then a threat, and finally a temptation. The fact that these connotations exist for this social stratum illustrates the extent to which the concept has been misrepresented. The elites view populism as a boogeyman, considering it to have humored the worst impulses in the masses. In this regard, de Benoist follows the Italian sociologist Federico Tarragoni, who sees the term "populism" as something of a verbal amulet which confers magical properties on its user, allowing him to discredit and socially condemn everyone to whom he applies it.

To take one illustrative example, the 2016 British referendum which concluded in favor of Brexit was viciously condemned by the liberal French philosopher Bernard-Henri Lévy, who held the event up as proof that the lowest sort of "rancid sovereignty" and "cattle nationalism" was ascendent in Western politics. Jacques Attali, taking a slightly different tone, viewed the referendum as a "Dictatorship of Populism"; Alain Minc, in turn, called it a "victory of the stupid over sensible people." What the intellectual establishment was criticizing was nothing less than the politics of the will of the people. The protagonists of Brexit were condemned and ostracized simply because they had complied with the majority's wishes. The interpretations of the results were even more surprising. The elderly voters were shunned for having voted for Brexit, while the younger generation were praised for having polled for progress. Jean Quatremer, for example, evinced anti-democratic sentiments when he decried the "dictatorship of the majority," implicitly advocating for a dictatorship of the minority. This anti-democratic direction was also reflected in the proposed solutions of the pro-EU camp. For example, European values ought to be excluded from future referenda, the elite opinion went, while the majority quorum in such referenda should be increased to as much as 90%. The people were suddenly being regarded as an internal enemy of the state as a result of their disobedience to their social masters. In this light, the class hatred of the elites became evident: to ask them whom they represented was unnecessary at best, and dangerous at worst, especially in the event that their allegiances lay elsewhere.

De Benoist observes the shift in mood that occurred after the British referendum, and how it cleared the way for curtailments on voting rights. As he insists, the pathologizing of the people was unfair, since the great catastrophes of history have more often than not stemmed from failure at the top, not at the bottom. This does little, however, to dissuade the elites from their attitudes, since their aim is merely to interdict any opposition to themselves, and to lie to the people. What necessarily results is their sawing off of the branch upon which representative democracy is perched. Yet, to stigmatize the populist impulse is, at once, to undermine the very foundation of democracy constituted by the people.

The source of this elite hatred of the people (the national ethnos) can be located in the Enlightenment era. While Machiavelli was still conjuring the ideal of the free citizen, the aim of the Enlightenment was to manipulate the youth with so-called "education." Since then, an aversion to the people has developed on the Right, which even allowed Joseph de Maistre to speak of the "Sovereign Tyranny of the People," the solution to which must be reforms imposed from above. Liberals, on the one hand, considered the simple people dangerous and tried to restrict the right to vote only to the rich. The Bonapartists, on the other hand, called for a return to the plebiscitary tradition of ancient Athens, despite its anti-parliamentarianism and anti-liberalism. Consequently, an opposition emerged between the sovereignty of parliament and the sovereignty of the people. With the emergence of Boulangism in 1889 came the idea that the head of state should be determined by free and direct general presidential elections, since his legitimacy can be affirmed only by the people. We find this tradition later on in the discourse of Gaullism. The principle of popular sovereignty also demands a rejection of supranational institutions like the European Human Rights Council since, in France, violence emanates from the people. In Western democracies, however, the popular sovereignty is replaced by a parliamentary sovereignty. Instead of pursuing the interests of the people, this aggregative democracy operates in accordance with the preponderance of private interests. Hence, the ministers of this system oppose referenda and direct democracy.

By respecting the interests of the individual, but not those of the people as a collective, liberalism tries to suppress popular participation in political decisions as much as possible. At the end of this development, the people's right to make decisions is replaced by the administration of assets, the sovereignty of financial markets, the authority of experts, and the government of judges. The system turns into an oligarchy which is unaccountable to anyone except for competing private interests. In this scheme, the people are left powerless. But the political competence of the technocrats proves itself to be no more than a myth. Democracy usually prioritizes politics over economics, the latter being a bulwark for the oligarchs, financial markets, and multinational corporations in the West. Here, de Benoist sees the Platonic ideal of "philosopher kings" who govern the ignorant people. The only legitimacy to which the technocratic elite can lay claim is to be found in their alleged competence to rule. If in the world of business, competence implies expertise, then in politics it is characterized by the simple ability to decide, the decision in question being self-sufficient, regardless of its content. The competence of the experts lies in offering recommendations, but not in determining policy. Thus, populism turns against expert ministers and election rituals, recognizing in them a deception of the people. After all, the people are able to decide what is politically good and bad for them, "good" and "bad" being entirely dependent on their preferences, rather than on some immutable truth. So, when an expert speaks of the incompetence of the people, it is because he confuses political problems with technical deficiencies and makes the case for the disempowerment of politics. Thus, liberal thought unmasks itself. Its main rationale is, as Margaret Thatcher said, that "there is no alternative."

This uniformity of mind ultimately leads to "singular thinking" (*Einheitsdenken*). Technocracy thus leads to the death of politics, as the general technical culture abolishes the conflicting interests and thereby nullifies the relevance of the political. By disseminating the idea that most negative phenomena are inevitable, technocracy negates the political and reduces it to mere administration. It is for this reason that the public accepts such atrocities as mass immigration — the tide and necessity of these phenomena seem inevitable and insuperable. The defamation of populists as "anti-progressive" by the intellectual class directly leads to a conferral of authority to the "experts" and "technicians" who, for their part, could not care less about the people's interests. In this sense, one should note the sharp divide between the "knowledgeable" and the "ignorant." Today, all kinds of people are called populists, be they Mao and Gaddafi or Trump, Orban, and Le Pen. Populism becomes a throwaway, all-inclusive term, a complex epithet encompassing the widest array of phenomena. In political science, however, populism is either described as an ideology (Ludovico Incisa di Camerana) or as a political style that can be applied to almost any ideological context (Pierre-André Taguieff). In 1981, Margaret Canovan went so far as to develop a typology of populism, separating it into the sub-categories of "protest populism," "national populism," and many other forms.

Of interest is how Alain de Benoist identifies the roots of populism in the United States and Russia, where it was characterized by the mobilization of the masses against the then ruling elites. The Russian case is exemplified by the movement of the *Narodniki*, which shaped political events between the 1860s and 1880s. They understood themselves to be Russian socialists who stood by the people and advocated for the development of a socialistic agrarian economy and increasing peasant literacy rates. Moreover, they advanced Russia's cultural self-determination and rejected Westernization. Unlike the later Bolsheviks, they did not regard the proletariat, but rather the peasantry as the sole revolutionary class, and they promoted the ideal of the rural community (known in Russian as the *obshchina* [община]). Their main representatives were Alexander Herzen, Dmitri Pisarev, and Nikolai Chernyshevsky. Likewise, In the US, Oliver Hudson Kelley founded the "Grangers" movement, whose proponents called for an end to financial speculation and mass industrialization, as well as social rights and the autonomy of small producers. The People's Party, founded in 1891 in Saint Louis by James B. Weaver and Thomas E. Watson, narrowly failed to seize executive power, as its candidate for the 1896 presidential election, William Jennings Bryan, lost to William McKinley by a scant margin of 1,600 votes. In contrast to the Russian Narodniki, who limited themselves to defending rural life against capitalism, the American Grangers also attacked finance capitalism. It is worth noting here that a hostility to progress was particularly characteristic of these early manifestations of populism. Populism can therefore be classified as neither left- nor right-wing, since it has not always advocated for the same position in relation to the antipodes of centralization/decentralization, Right/

Left, liberalism/anti-liberalism. Consequently, there can be no question of a common populist ideology.

Taking this into account, de Benoist endeavors to make an offer to the peoples in crisis: a populism of the people. Because this form of populism does not propose to create a "new man," one may describe it, in line with Ernesto Laclau, as ideologically neutral. Contrary to fascism, de Benoist declares his support for democracy, which can be identitarian (i.e., set in some relation to "identity"), even though not all identitarians are populists. Likewise, identitarian populism is different from national populism, since "identity" and "nation" do not always coincide. The chief characteristic of populism is that it is fundamentally directed against the elites. Since the Right often hastens to defend the elites, it is not always congruent with populism. Rather, the Right is fundamentally "elitist" insofar as its proponents believe that the people cannot govern themselves. Moreover, a traditional Right that mainly criticizes democracy is incompatible with a populism that demands more democracy. So, is it justifiable to see populism as a style rather than an ideology? The stylistic level of populism is evinced by its appeal to the people and their direct relationship to the government. Hence, the presence of a leader is not absolutely necessary for populism. Many populist movements do turn to one, but they do not necessarily have to be coupled to one. It is important that populist functionaries always present themselves as alike the ordinary man, without appearing divorced from or superior to him.

Another important characteristic of populism is its distinction from demagogy. Whoever equates populism and demagogy, de Benoist argues, forgets that there can also be a demagogy of the elites. In the Brexit debate, for example, we can observe that demonizing populism automatically leads to demonizing the people. Furthermore, the elites are fueling a debate that is designed to lead to the depersonalization of politics. As a matter of course, the state comes under a purely technical governance, a pure administration of things in which political debate is no longer relevant or even possible. If only "moral" or technical questions determine the discussion, there is no longer any room for polarizing opinions. This constitutes aggression against the majority, since their ability to make political decisions is voided. On this point, de Benoist quotes Vincent Coussedièrem, who pointed out that, without politics, there can be no people, nor can there be a people without politics. Populism, however, is presented by its opponents as a threat to democracy because it stands up for the whole people, while representative democracy emphasizes the differences. Accordingly, the question arises as to whether the people are just an illusion or whether populism is inextricably linked with the people and the idea of democracy. Since democracy has always self-identified as a form of government based on the sovereignty of the people, it requires the approval or consensus of its citizens. In a democracy, the people are sovereign in their social output; but, at the same time, democracy is also that form of government which guarantees the greatest possible participation of the public in deciding on public matters. Universal suffrage does not imply the right of the majority, but rather the individual ability to determine preferences. It is not majority status, the right to vote, elections, or representation that are decisive for democracy, but rather participation in governmental decisions. Arthur Moeller van den Bruck's dictum that "democracy is the participation of a people in its fate" should be the correct understanding, de Benoist argues. The real enemies of democracy, then, would not be the populists, but the supporters of "inadequate" democracy (representative democracy) in its regression to oligarchy. Populism, therefore, is an unmasking of the crisis of representative democracy and its democratic deficit.

By extension, populism's answer to the legitimacy crisis is the restoration of the people's sovereignty. But what are the dimensions of popular populism? According to de Benoist, three different facets can be distinguished here: (1) the political people (*demos*), (2) the people defined by their history and culture (*ethnos*), and (3) the people of the common classes (*plebs*). While *demos* describes populism in the political sense, *ethnos* describes its pre-political roots. In addition, *ethnos* is also the essential element of a people's identity and social behavior. Bourgeois nationalism, on the other hand, refers to abstract and universal principles. The people as *plebs* in the sense of the anti-elite masses is an important part of populism. Thus, on the one hand, populism unites all three approaches to and of the people while, on the other hand, it tries to embody all three at the same time. This explains why populists can be identified both as the representatives of "good" (democrats and progressives) and "bad" (racists and reactionaries). Nevertheless, it is difficult to distinguish between social populism and national populism, since the majority of populists combine both approaches. Finally, a common sociability is characteristic of the people. This, according to de Benoist, differentiates populist sociability from that of the state. Popular sociability is not the result of "one identity," but is based on traditions which act as the standard of what one has in common with the collective. Populism raises the restoration of a common world to its implicit goal of a common public space between people (Hannah Arendt). Furthermore, it is to be understood as a reaction to the decomposition of the people and their foundations. Faced with the developments of globalization and mass immigration, the people demand the right to continue to exist as nations. This, according to Ortega y Gasset, is the most basic and legitimate "human right"—the continued existence of one's people. The elite's never-ending fear-mongering over populism is thus revealed to be unfounded. In a society which has become angst-inducing, the people's fears cannot be trivialized as mere phantasms. Not least because of this, left-wing populism is taken far more seriously by social democrats, left-wing radicals, and the Green Party. Following de Benoist's train of thought, it is therefore up to the New Right to formulate a true populism of the people, an alternative which will overthrow the liberal elite and restore the people's sovereignty.

Arch-Enemy or Outcome of Liberalism?
The New Right's Views on Islam

EVER SINCE the events of September 11, 2001, the religion of Islam has taken on the image of "the enemy" for many right-wing groups. This perception redoubled in the wake of the attack on the liberal satirical magazine *Charlie Hebdo* in 2015 and the 2016 Christmas market attack at Breitscheidplatz in Berlin. Groups resembling "Islam critics" have begun to take shape across Europe, mirroring the activities of the American neoconservatives as well as their warning of an inevitable conflict between Islam and the "Enlightened West." Such European formations had an upswing in the wake of the US-sponsored "Arab Spring" of 2011 and have been growing in response to the progressive Islamization of Europe driven by regime-change wars in the Middle East and EU open-border policies. On one side of the issue are right-wing critics of Islam, such as Henryk Broder and Michael Ley, who see Islam as "the Enemy" and the greatest threat to Europe; this faction even includes figures like the German historian Egon Flaig, who suspects Islam of pursuing world domination. On the other side are representatives of the New Right, such as Alain de Benoist, Thor von Waldstein, and the Institute for State Policy (*Institut für Staatspolitik*; IfS) who, inspired by Samuel Huntington's "Clash of Civilizations" thesis, pose the question of whether the situation is not inadmissibly simplified when Islam is so uncritically vilified.[1]

---

1   Institut für Staatspolitik, *Ist der Islam unser Feind? Eine Lageanalyse. Wissenschaftliche Reihe — Heft 21* (2012; 2nd ed. 2015), 7.

After the end of the Ottoman Empire in the wake of its defeat in the First World War and the victory of the Kemalist Revolution under Kemal Atatürk, Islam returned to the geopolitical stage. But only in 1979, with the Islamic Revolution in Iran and the beginning of the successful Afghan Jihad against the Soviet Union, which went on until 1989, did Europeans become fully cognizant of the change that had occurred. The aim of this unadulterated Islam was and remains a total restoration of what it considers to be the canonical Islam of Prophet Mohammed.[2] This solution stems from the view that the political and economic inequalities the Islamic world faces *vis-à-vis* the West can be attributed to Muslims' rejection of pure Islam.

The criticism of Islam which arose as a reaction to this phenomenon is most visible today in the movement known as Patriotic Europeans Against the Islamization of the West (*Patriotische Europäer gegen die Islamisierung des Abendlandes*, PEGIDA), which has held regular demonstrations in Dresden and other cities in Germany since the end of 2014. Their five main critical theses against Islam can be summarized as follows:

1. The Problem is Islam.

2. There is no difference between Islam and Islamism.

3. There is an inherent pattern of Islamic aggression.

4. Islam forms a unity.

5. The goal of Islam is to Islamicize the world.[3]

This criticism of Islam implies that Islam is the main problem in Western societies. Its opponents insist that Islam tends to be structurally oppressive and violent. Muslims cannot unfasten themselves from the guidelines of their religion, and so are not integrable into Western societies. In this movement, Adolf Hitler's *Mein Kampf* and

---

2   Ibid., 11.

3   Ibid., 26.

the *Quran* are often compared with one another, which leads the discussion in this context to "Islamofascism." The IfS agrees with the statement that this tendency to reinterpret and disguise problems must be clearly criticized, it nonetheless rejects the idea that critics of Islam ultimately understand the religion in the same way that fundamentalist Muslims do. To criticize Islam as backward and in need of modernization is naïve, since it follows the dogma of Western development, according to which all societies have to develop in lockstep with the American model. Furthermore, the decisive problem of Islam does not lie in its religious character, but results from its identity-forming quality. Muslim teenagers cannot identify as Germans or French, nor even as Algerians or Arabs, but are Muslims above all else.

The second basic belief of these anti-Islamic groups is that there are no differences whatsoever between the religion of Islam and the political movement of Islamism. In the eyes of critics, the distinction is just a chess move made by EU authorities and their subordinate nations' leaders to calm unnerved Europeans. As proof, they have furnished cases in which seemingly "well-integrated" Muslims have carried out terror attacks in European countries. The IfS objects to the views of scholarly critics of Islam, such as Christine Schirrmacher, arguing that she and her ilk nonetheless adhere to the Islam/Islamism distinction. In the eyes of these scholars, Islamism is primarily a political, not a religious doctrine — a totalitarian ideology with a utopian worldview that is to be understood as an alternative to European modernity with its representative democracy and human rights. The majority of Islamic states are far from this form of Islam. Likewise, they claim, there is a spectrum in Islam that ranges from strict religious adherence to a more cultural Islam which hardly holds to the traditional "Five Pillars" of its theology.[4]

---

4   Ibid., 27–28.

The third point supposes a pattern of Islamic aggression. Here, the current mass immigration of Muslims into Europe is seen as the third wave of Islamic aggression, following the first wave which occurred under the prophet Mohammed and the second one under the auspices of Ottoman expansion.[5] Anti-Islamic sentiment is justified by the incoming Muslims' high birth rates, which could lead to a future Muslim majority in many European countries. But the IfS balks at this idea, insisting that mass immigration has never been a precept of Islamic conquest; rather, it is the liberal elite in European countries who have precipitated the conditions for mass demographic replacement. Muslim immigrants usually have individual motivations when they come to Europe, rather than doing so for the sake of the global Islamic community or *Ummah* [أمة]. Whereas some Islamic immigrants are highly susceptible to Islamist ideas, many are more or less assimilated, while another contingent of them simply live in a parallel society.

Fourth, the critics of Islam claim that the religion is a monolith, with immigrants in Europe functioning as the forward outposts of Islamic civilization. But the IfS insists that the Islamic space in the Middle East is divided into three main groups (Turks, Arabs, and Iranians), who remain hostile to each other. Finally, the main thesis of anti-Islam critics is that the aim of Islam is to transform the world in its image. On this point, IfS argues that the Islamization of Europe is only possible with the help of European collaborators. If Islam were consciously threatening Europeans with extinction, we would see the mechanism of such a cataclysm playing out in the actions of individual Muslims, as well as special Islamic groups or structures. The fact that individual Muslims can be "internal enemies" is no longer denied even by official politics, but Islam itself does not form a potential

---

5   Ibid., 28.

fighting unit in the Schmittean meaning of the term, which would constitute enmity as such.[6]

In his "Theses on Islam," Thor von Waldstein deepens the New Right's understanding of the subject. He begins by observing that the peoples of Islam are connected to Europe through a spiritual legacy which has lasted for centuries in certain areas of the continent. Orient and Occident are symbiotic entities, not antitheses. The excellent diplomatic relations that Germany and Turkey have maintained and enjoyed are exemplary in this regard. From a historical perspective, von Waldstein traces the roots of Islamic radicalization — predominantly political and non-religious — to the second half of the 20th century. Thus, with their harshness and arrogance, British, Dutch, and French colonial rule from the 18th to the middle of the 20th century instilled hatred and feelings of inferiority in the subjugated nations from Indonesia to the Maghreb. American neo-colonialism has seamlessly followed this tradition, unconditionally supporting Israel as it runs roughshod over its regional neighbors. Moreover, there is the corrosive decadence of the West (by which von Waldstein obviously means liberalism), which is destroying the family, peoples, and religion, and whose destructive power Islam recognizes and resists.[7] The roots of Islamic terrorism are ultimately to be found in the injustices of the West. The war between Islamists and the anti-terrorism apparatus in Western countries is asymmetrical and exacerbated by the despair of individuals, such as the 16-year-old Palestinian who watches his family home get demolished by an Israeli bulldozer. But, according to von Waldstein, there are no legitimate reasons for why this hatred would entitle someone to murder innocent civilians. Whoever wishes to pass righteous judgement must ensure that the real cause of this hatred is identified and eliminated, if the killing is to come to an end. From its very beginning, the War on

---

6   Ibid., 35.

7   Thor von Waldstein, "*Thesen zum Islam*" in *Die entfesselte Freiheit. Vorträge und Aufsätze* (Antaios, 2017), 189.

Terror initiated by the United States aimed to saddle Europe with its own interests and to sever the natural connections between Europe and the North Mediterranean. After having been blessed with such a false ally for half a century, Europe is now being made to suffer the incursion of what it wrongfully perceives as its enemy — Islam. After campaigns like "*Je suis Charlie*," this politically absurd animosity has advanced considerably.

Ultimately, in Thor von Waldstein's view, it is not only a misdeed, but an unforgivable mistake to fall hook, line, and sinker for the racism propagated in Western media against Europe's better geopolitical, intellectual, and cultural interests, supposing that Europe has more in common with the puritanically bigoted, spiritually dispossessed, and politically heteronomous white stockbroker in New York than it does with the non-white okra merchant from a bazaar in Cairo.[8] Much like the IfS, the author contradicts the idea of an Islamic conspiracy of mass immigration to Europe. This phenomenon is not a product of Islam, but rather the fruit of international capital and the liberal politics of guilt. The party responsible, contrary to the accusations of the German middle-class, includes figures such as Konrad Adenauer (1876–1967), Willy Brandt (1913–1992), Helmut Schmidt (1918–2015), Helmut Kohl (1913–1992), Wolfgang Schäuble, Gerhard Schröder, Angela Merkel, and other representatives of the German government who have supported mass immigration over the last several decades.

Following Alain de Benoist's position, Thor von Waldstein sees no way to integrate this influx of foreigners, since present-day Europe does not possess an identity into which one would care to integrate. Bearing this in mind, it is not surprising that young Turks and Arabs despise the West, while German women turn their backs on their effeminate men, emasculated by liberalism, and instead dream of non-Western men. Von Waldstein regards the churches in Europe as complicit in this defenselessness. While churches have mainly been

---

8   Ibid., 190–191.

devoted to proselytizing tolerance, overcoming the past, and granting church asylum, they forget their real task, which is to provide people support in faith and to provide for the possibility of transcendence. Thus, a self-inflicted religious vacuum emerged into which Islam was plunged. Germany and Europe today lack courageous churchmen like Benedict XVI, that rebel against the liberal dictatorship of relativism.[9] The expansion of Islam should therefore only be seen within the logic of proselytizing monotheistic religions, exacerbated by the failures of the European churches to offer a viable domestic option.

It is precisely through this perspective that von Waldenstein views the increase in the number of Muslims in Europe, which is largely taking place in maternity wards. Only after having expelled the alien American hegemon from its societies and having renewed its collaboration with Asia and northern Africa can Europe hope for a future. This also requires that Germany free itself of its pathological feeling of historical guilt. Otherwise, Europe cannot convince its citizens to procreate more than the immigrant population. Europe's only means of asserting itself in the 21st century is to pivot towards Asia while reducing its economic dependency on China, and to form a geopolitical alliance with Russia and the Mediterranean states. Here we can recognize Thor von Waldstein's Eurasian geopolitical orientation.[10]

Alain de Benoist finally undertakes to classify Islamism in terms of its history of ideas in the volume *The Roots of Hatred: An Essay on the Causes of Global Terrorism*. In this book, he emphasizes that Islamism is a product of modernity and, moreover, is not a new version of the religion, but draws on age-old Arab nationalism as well as the anti-imperialism of Arab culture. Furthermore, de Benoist writes, Islamism is an expression of disappointment in Arab nationalism, with its project of modernization based on the Western model, which failed to achieve technological and economic parity with the West.

---

9   Ibid., 192–193.

10   Ibid., 194–196.

The demand to return to a pure and original Islamic tradition first arose out of this disappointment.[11] At the same time, many Western commentators have outright yearned for Huntington's hypothesised "Clash of Civilizations" which, in the 21st century, would give rise to a dichotomy between Jihad and the "McWorld."[12] In view of this, de Benoist argues, Europeans must reject today's Western civilization and contemplate a multipolar world. In this conflict, one must refrain from holy war and from thereby becoming a tool of the Western liberal shopping mall. The liberal West has taken advantage of Islamic terror to achieve its designs, and the alternative presented by thinkers such as de Benoist is to reveal the global inequality, frustration, and despair that has resulted. Unfettered international capital and the seamless integration of social issues into the market economy are the main enemy, now more than ever.[13]

---

11 Alain de Benoist, *Die Wurzeln des Hasses. Ein Essay zu den Ursachen des globalisierten Terrorismus* (Berlin: Junge Freiheit, 2002), 46–48.

12 Ibid., 50.

13 Ibid., 57–58.

New Right Ecology: The Limits of Growth

THE TERM "climate change" is on everyone's lips nowadays. Ever since the effectively orchestrated mass media appearances of Greta Thunberg and the actions of "Extinction Rebellion," debates have been raging on issues such as environmental taxes and the reduction of CO_2 emissions. The Right has been unable to propose any solution to the dire environmental issues which Europe faces, nor has it proposed a new philosophy of life which could serve as a legitimate alternative to neoliberalism, other than its adoption of cosmetic, rote slogans like "Environmental care is care for the homeland" (*Heimatschutz ist Umweltschutz*). In the right-wing ecology postulated in the 2009 German edition of his book *Farewell to Growth*, Alain de Benoist postulates a culture of moderation combined with a radical critique of progress. Yet, why criticize progress and why say farewell to growth? De Benoist's answer is simple: a future without "degrowth" is impossible. With the emergence of the modern era, a radical rupture between man and nature occurred. Instead of understanding that, in modernity as in antiquity, human life has only been possible when man cared for his environment and, to paraphrase Cicero, planted trees that would benefit posterity, modern man instead began to callously exploit his living space.[1] Trapped in the logic of maritime civilization (Carl Schmitt), man has depleted an amount

---

1   Alain de Benoist, *Abschied vom Wachstum. Für eine Kultur des Maßhaltens* (Junge Freiheit, 2009), 26–27.

of resources in under 100 years that nature took 300 million years to develop.[2]

Western man's answer has been the idea of "sustainable" development. However, Alain de Benoist argues, this is merely a superficial solution, since it continues to regard nature as a fixed variable and allows for a further increase in the functional cost of the capitalist system, which remains committed to a continuous increase in production. Capitalism, which aims for infinite growth, denies the finitude of natural resources and, therefore, cannot be sustainable. As the proponent of degrowth Serge Latouche observes, the concept of sustainable development revolves around a deceptive idea, since the idea of limitless growth is not called into question, but is instead used to lull people into a false sense of security; this line of reasoning holds that the crisis can be resolved without challenging the logic of the markets, the economization of all areas of life, international finance, and capital itself.[3] So, instead of pursuing the false solutions of sustainable growth, growth itself must be reversed. This idea proposes an alternative in the form of a break with the previous societal model. The aim of degrowth is not turning back time, but rather proposing a new paradigm that expels consumerism and the primacy of the economy out of people's heads, which is alienating people from themselves.

As a consequence, it becomes more important to break with the things of the industrialized, modern world and rebuild the organic world of man. The destruction of the environment over the past 400 years has caused two simultaneous problems: on the one hand, the degradation of nature which has occurred due to pollution, and on the other hand, the scarcity of raw materials and resources.[4] According to de Benoist, this eventuality poses several threats to humanity. First, according to the discoveries of Charles King in

---

2   Ibid., 28.

3   Ibid., 29.

4   Ibid., 30.

1957, it will lead to an increase in carbon gases in the atmosphere. Seventy percent of emissions are caused by countries in the Northern Hemisphere. This increase in CO2 drives global warming, which in turn melts the Arctic ice sheets and raises the sea level. The Arctic ice sheets are expected to melt completely by 2070. This would just be one of the many environmental disasters caused by global warming. As a further consequence, catastrophic environmental events have been on the rise since 1969, occurring with a frequency that would have been spread out over several centuries prior to the industrial revolutions. Large forest fires caused by global warming have led to a decline in forested areas, which in turn has decreased the earth's ability to absorb the CO2 being released into the atmosphere, which then causes further warming of the planet and its attendant increase in natural disasters.[5]

The scarcity of resources is illustrated by the term "global oil peak." This is understood to be the peak after which the declining petroleum output cannot be compensated for by newer developments. The geologist and proponent of the peak oil theory Marion King Hubbert did indeed deliberately exclude unconventional oil production methods in his calculations, such as fracking, oil sands, etc. However, the global oil peak is already having geopolitical effects. It was one of the pretexts for the US invasion of Iraq and Afghanistan, as the United States wanted to expand their control over the oil-producing countries of the Middle East and Central Asia and bring the main shipping lanes under its control. This in turn has had a major impact on the US financial system, which greatly benefits from the petrodollar. It enables the US to accrue a large foreign trade deficit without having to live with the consequences of debt.[6] Alternative energy sources ultimately will not provide a way out of this dilemma — an energy source as cheap and energy-dense as oil is currently

---

5   Ibid., 31–35.

6   Ibid., 39–42.

inconceivable. If the economy continues down this track, Peter Barret prophesies the collapse of our current civilization as we know it well before the end of the 21st century.[7]

However, the proposed solutions for sustainable development are insufficient in the context of degrowth, and they merely reflect the current measures advocated by Western economists, mass media, and politicians. In the interest of sustainable development, prohibitions, regulatory measures, environmental taxes, and incentives for more environmentally friendly behavior should be pursued, but the worldwide deterioration of the environmental situation can no longer be halted by such measures. Moreover, carbon markets have only led to the creation of a new market, without ending environmental degradation. All such measures have followed the same logic, their assumption being that nature can be replaced by capital at will. Since the preconditions for human survival are invaluable, the costs of their destruction would be immeasurable, de Benoist emphatically argues. Consequently, no form of capital will ever be able to replace non-renewable energies. In addition, should we continue down this path, the autonomy of the Political will be abolished and replaced by an "expertocracy," an outcome on which the proponents of environmental sustainability place their hopes. To paraphrase Michel Serres, their measures resemble those of a captain whose ship is heading towards the rocks and who, in order to avert the catastrophe, proposes a reduction in speed instead of a change in course.[8] This kind of catastrophic myopia is based on a certain kind of global Western chauvinism, according to which the model of Western development is elevated to a universally applicable framework, to be applied to all the world's nations with minimal, locally-oriented adjustments. The developmental paradigms of the globally dominant West are ultimately a continuation of colonization by other means, since the

---

7   Ibid., 43–45.

8   Ibid., 49–55.

West's cultural hegemony reaches its fullest extent when its targets are at their most politically vulnerable. By means of such developmental paradigms (such as "development economics"), which preach unlimited growth and claim the ability to satisfy a likewise unlimited expansion of desires, the idea of a borderless, nationless globe is also advanced. Thus, non-Western peoples are forced into a vicious circle, obliged to adhere to the liberal dictum. Liberals have presumed that if a resource were to become scarce, its price would correct itself upwards to reflect supply, and demand would automatically fall. But if a lifestyle inevitably depends on the constant supply of certain resources, the demand for these resources can be neither curtailed, nor substituted. The people dependent on it surrender themselves to their addictions, willing to resort to any means to satisfy their cravings.[9]

In order to find a way out of this vicious circle, the advocates of degrowth call for divorcing the religion of growth and the monotheism of the market. Their theories go back to the early 1970s, to the United Nations' Environmental Conference in Stockholm and the 1972 Meadows Report entitled *The Limits to Growth* delivered at the Club of Rome, where the presenters demanded a reversal in the economy. As the environmental situation was reaching an even further state of degradation by the early 1990s, these demands were revisited. In their political propaganda, members of the degrowth movement insist on the truism that, without an end to the mania of growth, humanity will inevitably go extinct. The means of avoiding this potential future, then, would be a snuffing out of individual egoism and an emphasis on frugality. For de Benoist, however, such sermons can only hope to move a very few hearts; greed and egoism are not the exclusive fruits of modernity, after all, but have existed for as long as man has. Perhaps egoism cannot be eliminated from oneself, but the ideology of liberalism, which elevates egoism to its highest principle, can be addressed. Serge Latouche's proposed "disaster

---

9   Ibid., 56–61.

education" would also not lead to a paradigm shift, as the prospect of disaster has historically led people to wars, but without ever fundamentally reforming society. Instead, the discourse of degrowth can initiate a paradigm shift in the minds of men, bringing into question the dominance of the economy over all areas of life.[10] In practical terms, according to Edward Goldsmith, a leader in the movement, we could avoid a major climate crisis if we were to reduce production and consumption each year over a period of ten years. Yet, because people can hardly be convinced to sacrifice their wealth at the current juncture, and because a political solution seems impossible, the question remains as to how this crisis can be overcome.[11]

Alain de Benoist states that degrowth cannot provide a complete solution to this question. The only way in which society can overcome such an ecological challenge is to redefine what constitutes a high standard of living. Consumption numbs the sensorial experience and makes us rather stingy in terms of sociability, atrophying good-neighborly relationships, denying us a stress-free life, and deteriorating our notions of beauty.[12] In short, de Benoist argues, we need a different standard of living. The increase in obesity in the West, for example, is just a symbol of our insatiability and slavery to consumption and profit. Against this hubris, ecology could propose *phronesis*, or the virtue of prudence which seeks to establish a harmonious balance.[13] According to de Benoist, the greatest task ahead for the ecological cause consists not only in presenting a critique of growth, but also in posing greater questions concerning the purpose of our existence and presenting an image of man that would be ethically and metaphysically capable of preventing environmental degradation and of ending galloping productivism. In short, this new image of man

---

10   Ibid., 88.

11   Ibid., 90.

12   Ibid., 92.

13   Ibid., 93.

will be a rallying cry against the ideology of the Enlightenment, of Modernity.[14]

In order to get there, Benoist insists that we must radically redefine our values and understandings in two areas. Firstly, we require a robust critique of progressive thought; secondly, we must reconnect with nature. De Benoist defines the key concept of progress as the notion that every innovation is good just because it is new. Accordingly, history is presumed to be moving invariably toward a more perfect state: while the world in its current state is imperfect, it can be perfected through human intervention. The ultimate outcome of the steady march of progress is supposed to be paradise on earth. While the differences between nations are considered only temporary conditions within universal history, the more developed societies are tasked with helping with the development of the less developed societies. The advancement of progress is measured in terms of material prosperity which, as de Benoist notes, is not sufficient to establish a high standard of living, since it excludes the social dimension.[15] The danger of progressivism is its implicit claim to being the way and law of nature as it sanctions a total liberation from all traditional worldviews. Only after having unfettered himself from tradition can man become human in the modern sense. The paradigm of progress then comes to regard traditional man as inhuman, or even subhuman. In this way, the ideologies of progress establish a racism in the world which causes a deep rift between primitive/non-rational peoples and advanced civilizations.[16] Thereby, (Western) man draws a circle of increasingly exclusive humanism around himself which not only marginalizes, stigmatizes, and isolates more and more people—a treatment which has historically been a prelude to genocide—but also regards the environment as nothing more than a commodity to

14   Ibid., 96.

15   Ibid., 102.

16   Ibid., 104–105.

be used, resulting in his total alienation from nature and all other life existing on the planet. The task of the environmental movement consists in convincing people to acknowledge the limitations of Earth's resources and overcome the separation between man and nature so as to restore an arrangement of mutual cohabitation. It is not a question of whether man should rule over nature, or nature over man, but rather whether man can once again assume his task as a "shepherd of being" (Heidegger).[17]

Environmental critique is, therefore, a logical building block in de Benoist's holistic thinking and an important impetus for the New Right to rethink borders in ecological terms and not just in terms of immigration and geopolitics. After its fears have materialized — namely that capitalism would instrumentalize the environmental movement to its purposes — the New Right has come to view environmental issues and degrowth as pressing matters, which must go beyond slogans such as "Environmental care is care for the homeland" if ecology is not to be relinquished to be the sole domain of the Left. In order to address this problem, one must be prepared to question the axioms of capitalism and its growth-focused economic paradigms, which are more important to the liberal Right than the continued existence of one's own homeland.

---

17   Ibid., 113.

Imperium or Nation-State?
The New Right's Critique of Nationalism

THE NATION and the nation-state are two concepts on the Right that are considered almost unassailable. All the more interesting in this context are Alain de Benoist's reflections on the nation-state, which he develops in his essay "The Imperial Idea: The Model for the Future Structure of Europe" published in the volume *A Beautiful Interconnected World: A Response to Globalization*.[1] The French philosopher begins by tracing the genesis of *Imperium* and nation and concludes by explaining why *Imperium*, or Empire (German *Reich*), is an alternative to the nation-state.

De Benoist argues that there are two major models of political unity discernible in Europe's political history: the nation-state and the *Imperium*, or Empire. After the collapse of the Roman Empire, symbolically marked by the deposition of its last emperor, Romulus Augustulus (460–507), in 475, the West would not see another emperor until the coronation of Charlemagne by Pope Leo III on December 25, 800. This "renewal of the empire of the Romans" (*renovatio imperii Romanorum*) applied the formula of the "transfer of rule" (*Translatio imperii*) which declared that the Roman Empire would find its continuation in the Empire of Charlemagne. This event put an end to the ongoing speculation about the biblical Daniel's prophecies of an impending end of the world following the fall of

---

1   Alain de Benoist, "Der Reichsgedanke. Das Modell für die zukünftige Struktur Europas" in *Schöne Vernetzte Welt. Eine Antwort auf die Globalisierung* (Hohenrain, 2001).

empire (the Roman Empire) in the West. The *renovation* of the empire brought about a divorce with the Augustinian notion of a radical separation between *civitas terrena* and *civitas dei,* which by then had led to the assumption that a Christian *Imperium* was an unattainable dream. With the imperial coronation of Charlemagne, the Pope introduced the idea that the emperor is the protector of the divine state. The emperor thus received the authority to exert power from the Pope, whose spiritual authority he replicated in the secular sphere. The later Investiture Controversy can be traced to the ambiguous formulation which made the emperor a subject of the ecclesiastical order but placed him at the head of a secular hierarchy with a sacred character.

In 843, the Frankish Empire was divided amongst Charlemagne's three grandchildren: Charles the Bald (823–877) acquired the western third of the Carolingian Empire, Louis the German (806/810–876) became the first king of East Francia, and Lothar I (795- 855) received Middle Francia between this two brothers' holdings.[2] The conditions for a new German-Roman Empire were met with the coronation of Henry the Fowler (876- 936) from the Ottonian dynasty, followed by the restoration of the Empire by Otto I (912- 973), who was crowned emperor in Old St. Peter's Basilica in Rome. The Ottonian and Salian dynasties built the empire into the leading power in Central Europe, dominating the continent until the middle of the 13th century. In 1254, this polity assumed the title of "Holy Roman Empire" (*Sacrum Romanum Imperium*) along with the phrase "of the German Nation" in 1442. The Empire combined three aspects: a provenance from antiquity, Christianity, and Germanness.

The dissolution of the imperial idea can in fact already be established in the Renaissance as the first nation-states emerged, even if this development was apparently reversed with the victory of the imperial army over Francis I "le Roi-Chevalier" ("the Knight-King,"

---

2   Ibid., 241–243.

1494–1547) at Pavia in 1525. However, the empire was reduced to its German part at the latest with the abdication of Emperor Charles V (1500- 1558) in 1556 and the ascension of Ferdinand I (1503–1564). The Peace of Westphalia from 1648 further reduced it to a mere union of territorial states. Its end was eventually sealed on April 6, 1806, when Napoleon completed the Revolution by dissolving the remnants of the empire. The Holy Roman Empire of the German Nation ceased to exist when Francis II (1768–1835) renounced the Roman-German Imperial crown.[3]

So much for the history of the empire—but what is its significance? The best way to define "Empire," according to de Benoist, is to differentiate it from the nation. In the Middle Ages, the latter term possessed only an ethnic meaning, designating, for instance, the various "national" student bodies which had been structured respectively in Paris, Bologna, and Prague. Even the term *Patria*, meaning "fatherland," which only emerged with the humanists of 16th-century France, originally signified "country" (*pays*). Politically, modern nation-building begins with the efforts of Philip II of France (1165–1223), who bore the title *Rex Francie* from the beginning of the 13th century. The idea of the nation was not coined completely until the 18th century, above all during the French Revolution. Originally, the idea of the nation referred to a formulation of sovereignty which differentiated itself completely from absolute monarchy, since it united those who were politically and philosophically like-minded. The nation then became an abstract *locus*, where people could articulate and exercise their rights, and individuals could be turned into citizens. From then on, it embodied the unity of the country and superseded the king. The nation, therefore, signifies the sovereign people, who endow the king with the authority to exert power in accordance with laws arising from the popular will. As for the people, the nation is a polity made up of citizens who acknowledge the authority of

---

3   Ibid., 244.

the state and view themselves as members of a single political unit. Accordingly, Article 3 of the *Declaration of the Rights of Man and of the Citizen* of 1789 proclaims that the principle of sovereignty essentially resides in the nation.

In this context, Bertrand de Jouvenel articulates that the goal of the Revolution was the establishment of a cult of the nation. When de Benoist subsequently makes a distinction between *Imperium* and nation, the latter term refers not only to the modern conception of the "nation-state," but also to the popular monarchism of the *Ancien Régime*, which prefigured the nation in many respects. *Imperium* or Empire, however, is primarily an idea and a principle, not a territory.[4] The essential component of the *Imperium* was the emperor, who did more than merely possess the state. As the "ruler of the world" (*dominus mundi*), he was suzerain and thus supreme feudal lord of both princes and kings; he ruled over rulers, not territories, and represented a power that transcended the community he led. Regarding rulership in *Imperium*, the distinction between the *auctoritas* (moral and spiritual superiority) and *potestas* (sheer public power) is important. In the medieval *Imperium*, this separation corresponded to the difference between the imperial function and authority on the one hand, and the authority which the emperor as ruling prince of a certain people held. To pay homage to the emperor was not to express devotion to a particular people or state. Likewise, patriotism was a bond between different peoples of the empire which outweighed national or religious ties.[5]

The Christian reinterpretation of the imperial idea in the Middle Ages resulted in the emperor being viewed as the executor of a holy universal history, and therefore the *Imperium* as a holy institution was called to wield independent power vis-à-vis the papacy. This conviction led to a dispute within the Holy Roman Empire between

---

4   Ibid., 245–246.

5   Ibid., 247.

the Ghibellines, loyal to the Emperor, and the Papist Guelphs. The Ghibellines opposed the Pope's claim to power by resorting to the age-old distinction between *Imperium* and *Sacerdotium* (or "Throne and Altar"), in which the two domains of power were seen to hold equal importance, both having been created by God. In light of this, spiritual authority was never subject to the secular, but rather the emperor was granted a spiritual authority of his own. The empire was to be recognized as a sacred institution just like the Church and the Papacy. The dispute between Ghibellines and Guelphs thus symbolized the conflict between two kinds of *dignitates*, both of which were rooted in the spiritual plane.[6]

The fall of the Empire was the result of its reduction to a purely territorial definition, since it could not turn into a nation without first falling into fragmentation. Without its spiritual superstructure, it would have degenerated into the purely violent institution of "imperialism," as Julius Evola noted. In their historical development, the Germans persevered the imperial tradition, while the French starting heading towards a nation-state already under Hugh Capet (939- 996).[7] Hence, in France, beginning in the 14th-15th centuries, territorial sovereignty began to oppose the emperor's spiritual authority over legal scholars, and centralism was promoted over the feudal nobility and civic life. Jean Bodin's theory of sovereignty from the 16th century ultimately had the goal of removing all of the king's obligations towards the emperor. In France, the nation-state emerged with the rise of centralism on the one hand and with the rise of the bourgeoisie on the other. When King Louis XVI proclaimed, "I am the state" ("*L'état, c'est moi*"), he meant that there was nothing superior to the state. Whereas, in France, the state brought the nation into being, and this in turn gave birth to the French people, other countries of the imperial tradition experienced the modern nation first

---

6   Ibid., 248.

7   Ibid., 249.

being formed by the people, which only then turned to formulate its statehood.

Hence, two fundamentally different historical constructions of the nation-state emerged, and this contrast explains the differences between Empire and nation.[8] This difference proceeded towards a different understanding of political unity. While a nation would create its own culture with which to underpin itself, and to create conditions of consensus between people and state, the *Imperium* would encompass multiple peoples with the aim of creating a unity of general and particular. Its highest guiding principle would be self-determination and respect for distinctiveness. *Imperium* would unite ethnicities and peoples without abolishing their cultural diversity. It would be a whole in which the individual parts would be more self-determined rather than being entirely conditioned by that which binds them together. These constituent parts would remain organically differentiated units. Hence, *Imperium* would rely more on peoples than on the state. Its endeavor would be to envision a common fate for a multiplicity of ethnoi, without merging them into a homogeneous soup. In this sense, the concept of *Imperium* corresponds to the classic image of *universitas* in contrast to the uniformly centralized *societas* of the national kingdoms. Whereas *Imperium* differentiates between ethnic affiliation and citizenship, this distinction was completely alien to the nation.[9]

Another point of difference between *Imperium* and nation is in the dichotomy between holism on one side and individualism and universalism on the other. According to de Benoist, the logic of the nation aims to abolish everything that it perceives as an obstacle between the central state and individuals. This logic determined the division of France into three equal estates during the French Revolution while ignoring historical national borders; the French

---

8   Ibid., 250–251.

9   Ibid., 252–253.

Republican government launched an offensive against regional languages and dialects, abolished region-specific laws, and standardized weights and measures. To put it succinctly, political uniformity was pursued and conformity was enforced. The individualistic characteristics of the nation can also be seen in the revolutionary centralization that made the state into a monopolistic producer of society. The nation only knows the individual and seeks to dismantle all intermediate structures in an attempt to guarantee the state's direct access to each individual. On the other hand, one only belongs to the *Imperium* indirectly, i.e., *via* intermediate bodies. In this regard, de Benoist cites Louis Dumont, who pointed out that nationalism leads exactly to the type of global society in which the rule of the individual is a self-sufficient value. Whereas, in the Middle Ages, one assumed a bipolar identity consisting of ethnicity and religion, the nation-state promoted the idea of a closed society in which only the state could bestow an identity upon its citizens.

The character of the nation as anti-*Imperium*, de Benoist maintains, can be illustrated through several clarifying examples: the Netherlands was born out of a divorce from the house of Habsburg, England could assert itself as a nation only after its conflict with Rome, and France could only rise to nationhood by way of clashing with the traditional forces of the whole of Europe.[10] The borders of the Holy Roman Empire were always fluid; this empire saw itself as universal, but not universalistic, and did not adhere to any idea of worldwide expansion. Furthermore, the concept of *Imperium* relates to the vision of a just order that strives to unite people on the basis of a concrete political order, beyond all proselytism and homogenization. Therein lies its distinction from both the idea of a world state and the idea that universally valid legal-political principles should exist for all times and places.

---

10   Ibid., 256–257.

De Benoist maintains that this political universalism can trace its origins to the individualistic roots of the nation-state. The case of French nationhood serves as a prime example, as it saw itself as the most universal of all nations. If the nation is oriented towards humanity, then humanity must be oriented towards the nation.[11] Those who resist are excluded not only from their respective nation, but more broadly from humanity *per se*. The Roman, Byzantine, Ottoman, and Holy Roman Empires were precisely such *Imperia*. By contrast, the Napoleonic Empire, the Third Reich, and the British Empire were nation-states. All great modern powers have been nations, as is evident from the fact that their expansion has not been based on a spiritual principle, but on sheer military force, which ultimately led to misfortune and disaster. Julius Evola went so far as to define an "empire" which does not follow the model of the holy *Imperium* as a cancerous growth inside a living organism.[12]

Given the dominance of the nation-state in the present international system, can the *Imperium* be considered an alternative at all, or is it a mere pipe dream? According to de Benoist, the Roman Empire is being discussed today as a way of overcoming the nation-state in the same manner as the imperial idea (Holy Roman Empire) stood behind the concepts that led to the building of a united Europe. The underlying impetus is the decline of the nation. The motives driving the world are increasingly extra-national. The nation-state is being called into question from below as well as from above. The new ties of community, regional, and autonomous movements, as well as new social currents, are calling nations into question at their very foundations, as the widening gap between civil society and the ruling political caste is leading to the proliferation of localized networks and tribalization. At some point, the nation-state came to be deprived of

---

11   Ibid., 257–258.

12   Ibid., 259–260.

its power from above by world markets, international institutions, the technoscientific apparatus, and intergovernmental bureaucracies.

Thus, Daniel Bell's assessment may be deemed accurate: the nation-state is too small to solve big problems, but also too big to solve small problems.[13] As an alternative to the national centralized state, de Benoist proposes a federally structured and anti-imperialistic *"Imperium Europa,"* referring to the concept of Middle Europe (*Mitteleuropa, Zwischeneuropa*) from the "Action Circle" (*Tatkreis*) of the Conservative Revolution.[14] This would resolve many problematic autonomy movements, as well as further facilitate revising the problematic relationship between citizenship and ethnicity against the backdrop of mass immigration. De Benoist concludes that the problem of the present lack of an imperial ideal could be resolved by taking the guiding principle to be the struggle for the sake of the diversity of the world against the homogeneity of liberalism.[15]

---

13   Ibid., 262–263.

14   Ibid., 265. By "anti-imperialistic," de Benoist means being against the secular nation-state's territorial expansion over and against other nation-states, which the post-Enlightenment nation-states pursued after their ties with the transcendence and sacrality of dominion had been severed, leaving only earthly domination.

15   Ibid, 269–270.

Ten Theses on Liberalism

THE GERMAN jurist Dr. Thor von Waldstein is regarded as one of the most eloquent representatives of the New Right in Germany. Born in Mannheim in 1959, he became a Doctor of Social Sciences in 1989, under the supervision of Bernard Willms (1931–1991), a well-known specialist on the writings of Thomas Hobbes (1588–1679), and in 1992, von Waldstein became a Doctor of Law at the University of Mannheim. In addition to his legal expertise in maritime law, he also served as a defense attorney in cases regarding the suppression of dissident freedom of expression in the Federal Republic of Germany. Among his other works, Von Waldstein has published two studies for the Institute for State Policy (*Institut für Staatspolitik*, IfS): *We Germans Are the People: On the Political Resistance of the Germans During the 'Refugee Crisis' according to Article 20 IV of the German Constitution* (2016)[1] and "Who Protects the Constitution before Karlsruhe: Critical Notes on Newer Case Laws of the Federal Constitutional Court concerning 'the Ethnic Concept of the People'"[2] (2017), as well as two volumes in the series *Kaplaken* (published by Antaios) entitled *Metapolitics:*

---

1   Thor von Waldstein, *Wir Deutsche sind das Volk — Zum politischen Wider-standsrecht der Deutschen nach Art. 20 IV Grundgesetz in der ‚Flüchtlingskrise', Wissenschaftliche Reihe* 28 (Verein für Staatspolitik, 2016).

2   Thor von Waldstein, *Wer schützt die Verfassung vor Karlsruhe: Kritische An-merkungen zur neueren Rechtsprechung des Bundesverfassungsgerichts betr. den ethnischen Volksbegriff, Wissenschaftliche Reihe* 34 (Verein für Staatspolitik, 2017).

Situation — Dream — Action[3] (2005) and *Power and the Public Sphere* (2018).[4] Von Waldstein also authored the preface to the new edition of *Socialism and Nation* [*Sozialismus und Nation*] (2019) by Hermann Heller (1891–1933), published by Jungeuropa.

In his "Ten Theses on Liberalism" (*Zehn Thesen zum Liberalismus*) published by Antaios in his volume of collected essays *Freedom Unleashed: Lectures and Essays against Liberal Oblivion*[5] (2017), the author presents a comprehensive critique which proceeds from the antithesis between liberalism and conservatism formulated by Hans-Dietrich Sander in his 1988 book *The Dissolution of all Things*.[6] While a person who no longer feels himself to be part of a community is characterized as a self-obsessed liberal, the conservative man is marked by his selflessness, his adherence to the holiness of a cause that does not die with him. Liberal man, on the contrary, would surrender all matters to the deluge. Thus, conservatism builds upon the strengths of man, whereas liberalism appeals to his weaknesses. Beginning with this thesis of Sander's, Waldstein claims that liberalism is "anti-social." In contrast to other worldviews (*Weltanschauungen*) which endeavor to connect people, liberalism makes use of every means to absolve man of his collective commitments. Instead of compensating for the shortcomings of "deficient being" (*Mängelwesens*), to paraphrase Arnold Gehlen, the liberal order seeks to isolate its individual subjects so that they are softened and easily manipulated by the state.[7] According to liberal doctrine, man is a self-sufficient individual only when dislocated as a social atom. From a Traditionalist understanding of the world, however, as in the

---

3   Thor von Waldstein, *Metapolitk. Lage — Traum — Tat* (Antaios, 2005).

4   Thor von Waldstein, *Macht und Öffentlichkeit* (Antaios, 2018).

5   Thor von Waldstein, *Die entfesselte Freiheit. Vorträge und Aufsätze wider die liberalistische Lagevergessenheit* (Antaios, 2017).

6   Hans-Dietrich Sander, *Die Auflösung aller Dinge: Zur geschichtlichen Lage des Judentums in den Metamorphosen der Moderne* (1988).

7   von Waldstein, *Die entfesselte Freiheit*, 159.

case of the Conservative Revolutionary Othmar Spann, man can be free and develop himself only when he is part of a community, where he can bring his personality and moral nature to maturity in unity with other people. In doing so, man does not lose his independence and inner freedom, since each member of the community has a life of his own, and the whole cannot exist without its parts.[8] The man believed to be free in liberalism is, in truth, subject to laws which foreclose on communality. As the Swiss Federal Constitution already insightfully stipulates, only those who demand their freedom can be free. In liberalism, however, man is delivered to the anarchy of everyday life. Without connection to the community, the individual perishes.[9]

Secondly, liberalism lacks any sense of the representative. Western democracies also celebrate national holidays, but the negative memorial days predominate, such as those commemorating the crimes of colonialism or fascism. The pride of guilt takes the place of the national pride.[10] Such a state cannot but be short lived, and this is by design. As Alexander Dugin has already argued, the nation-state was created by the bourgeoisie in order to enlighten their fellow citizens — but only to the extent that they can then be dissolved within global civil society. Waldstein's third thesis is that liberalism is libertarian, not liberal. In a totalitarian manner, liberalism is mercilessly on the offensive against all those whom it perceives as "enemies of freedom." Whoever transgresses against the mass-media-established limits on the freedom of expression, whether in the sphere of foreign policy (integration with the West) or domestic politics (remigration), gets socially ostracized. As conventional wisdom states, he who is born in a thought prison comes to love his servitude. According to Waldstein, what contemporary society lacks are courageous young

---

8   Ibid., 161.

9   Ibid., 162.

10   Ibid., 163.

men who will not allow themselves to be swayed by public opinion because they value the lives of their grandchildren more than their own. Our post-heroic society lacks any creative anger, having become insensitive to everything, and thus cannot ensure our children's future.[11] While liberalism shows appreciation and demands the greatest possible liberties for its "sheltered minorities" (*Hätschelminderheiten*), from gays to Roma, it takes a radical totalitarian stance against all perceived objectors. There is no "freedom for the heterodox" — only a freedom of and for those who think alike.

Moreover, Waldstein diagnoses a certain kind of parasitism: liberalism feeds on foundations which it is incapable of creating on its own. Liberal society is defined by its formlessness, dominated by egomaniacs without any sense of duty or responsibility, who attempt to mask their own hollowness with mottos such as, "You only live once." Von Waldstein's contends that those whose identities are solely produced by their consumption patterns and leisure habits cannot preserve any state. The liberal state will inevitably crumble. When it does, it threatens to drag its hostage populations into the abyss with it. Hence, according to Willy Hellpach, a liberal state is as absurd a proposition as a burning block of ice.[12]

In his sixth thesis, von Waldstein argues that the essence of liberalism is its penchant for unending debate. The aim of such "government by discussion" is to sustain a constant, debilitating argument which must never yield a conclusion. The difference between this "show debate" and a show trial is one of only the slightest degree, claims Botho Strauss. In this schema, the media-ruled public conforms to a bloodless tyranny which need not cause heads to roll in order to achieve its aims. Since there are no longer any political actors, there is no longer any need to distinguish between friend and foe, given that there are only participants and conformists within

---

11　Ibid., 165.

12　Ibid., 167.

the system.[13] Those who remain silent are in consent, and surrender themselves completely to the regime. If any discussion ever does occur in the liberal model, then it focuses on non-sensitive issues, and is never followed by action. As a consequence, the countless corpses in the basement of the liberal system are deliberately ignored. The family is dissolved, abortions rise to the level of an epidemic, the rule of law is gradually dismantled in favor of organized criminals, and all the while a total silence is imposed. If ever these issues were to inhabit the center of public consciousness, they would disrupt the bread-and-circus liberal culture.[14] Unending, soporific debates have the purpose of silencing critical issues from receiving serious treatment. The result is a tabloid republic of taboos, in which individuals consumed by vanity can publicly discharge their opinions on non-pressing issues provided that nothing changes.[15]

In his seventh thesis, von Waldstein accuses liberalism of being based on a perverted concept of freedom. Freedom is mistaken for an indulgent lack of restraint, a disengagement from all commitments. This also gives rise to the liberal worldview's internal alienation from the state. The man with deep roots, on the other hand, always understands freedom as the room for maneuvering that he requires for his own existence within the overall life of his *ethnos*, allowing for his filiation with God. He does not long for freedom because he regards the individual as the highest value, to whom all restrictions must be removed in favor of lower types of values, but, to the contrary, he demands freedom because he sets the individual in service of higher values, and because he must be able to develop his personality in order to fulfil this duty.[16] Besides, the liberal is characterized by his inability and disinclination to sacrifice himself for a higher ideal. The

---

13   Ibid., 168.

14   Ibid., 169.

15   Ibid., 170.

16   Ibid., 172–173.

liberal only revolves around his own axis, installs himself comfortably in his leisure- and consumption-pod, severing all connections to his history and culture. The hatred of liberal society is therefore directed against all those who acknowledge their history and tradition and strive to continue their generational succession, refusing to allow their dignity to be stripped from them by the endless spectacle of consumer society. This ultimately means bearing children and educating them in the spirit of their parent's heritage. This characteristic clearly demonstrates that the tyranny of freedom is an unleashed freedom.

In his eighth thesis, von Waldstein states that liberalism and democracy are mutually incompatible. The people, as a collective, cannot have sovereignty if only the individual is granted rights. In the Federal Republic of Germany, for instance, there is never a vote when it comes to the most important issues. Von Waldstein cites the following events as illustrative of this state of affairs: the accession to NATO in 1955, the waves of immigration since the 1960s, the elimination of the Deutsche Mark, the accession to the Nuclear Non-Proliferation Treaty, the abandonment of the ethnic concept of peoplehood, the annexation of the German Democratic Republic by the German Federal Republic instead of a veritable unification, the rescue packages to save the Eurozone, and the illegal opening of the borders in 2015 that resulted in the smuggling of masses of migrants. The latter are more than enough evidence of the actual state of "for-show democracy."[17]

Regarding capitalism, there is a reciprocal relationship between it and liberalism. Liberalism's destruction of the established order prepares the field for the monetary rule of capitalism. The economic success of capitalism in turn constitutes the crucial basis for the political success of liberalism. For this reason, liberalism appeals to the lowest

---

17   Ibid., 173.

instincts of man, namely licentiousness and incontinence.[18] Von Waldstein thus arrives at his ninth thesis, which holds that liberalism and capitalism are Siamese twins. Though liberalism cannot resolve the political contradictions within society on its own, it nevertheless attempts to drown them in prosperity by projecting individualistic imperatives, such as "Enrich yourself!" and "Have fun!" Admittedly, money is an effective way to keep society running, but it can never constitute an acceptable claim to power for men.[19] And this is exactly the Achilles heel of the political system: for better or worse, it is condemned to require infinite economic growth and prosperity.

The economic crisis ongoing since 2008 has made it plain that capitalism has likely reached the end of its tether. Whether we have already reached a pre-revolutionary phase or not, von Waldstein dares not say. As the money system stands before an impending collapse, capitalism can neither prevent ethno-religious conflicts in Europe from escalating, nor hide its anti-social structure in the face of economic decline. An end to plutocracy could soon be at hand. Nonetheless, we continue to live under the rule of the "debased" (*Minderwertigen*) embodied by liberalism. Western democracy upholds a deliberately negative system of selection through the party system: our political class does not embody an elite of moral integrity, but rather one of schemers, liars, and deceivers. Consequently, von Waldstein concedes, one can only hope that a healthy opposition force will not engage the waning rule of the debased on the latter's own terms, but rather that it will assert itself on a completely new principle — which is so desperately needed in a Germany contaminated by liberalism.[20]

With his ten theses on liberalism, Thor von Waldstein presents a relevant critique of this insidious ideology, revealing its true

---

18   Ibid., 174.

19   Ibid., 175.

20   Ibid., 176.

intentions and harmful consequences. In a similar manner to Alain de Benoist, he emphasizes the fact that liberalism as a modern ideology shares roots with communism, but that liberalism is the fundamental evil. It is no coincidence that Karl Marx articulated his thought in the middle of 19th-century London, then the largest banking center in the world, as well as ground zero of colonial capitalism. Communist movements did not arise in vacuum, but could only have thrived on the desolate soil left in the destructive wake wrought by the capitalist and liberal disregard for human communality.[21]

---

21 Ibid., 174.

Beyond Human Rights

Beyond Human Rights — thus reads the title of Alain de Benoist's 2004 book, published in German as *Critique of Human Rights* (*Kritik der Menschenrechte*), which fundamentally questions the eponymous Western article of faith.[1] In this text, de Benoist grapples with the philosophical background of the West's secular religion. The main critique de Benoist levies against human rights is that they involve a universalism which distorts objectivity, deriving "is" from "ought."[2] This way of thinking stems from an abstraction of the world, not an objective view of things. The error is the result of a symmetrical reversal of the false assumption that good as such coincides with the good for oneself or one's own community. Because of this, de Benoist believes, universalism directly contradicts the European tradition, which is always defined by a struggle against unrestrained subjectivity.[3]

Today, we are experiencing a hegemony of human rights which threatens to substitute all political and social discourses, which in turn are in danger of lapsing into illegitimacy just as tradition and the nation already have. This is due not least to human rights serving as a the pretence for a world government. Thus, as early as 1776, the American Declaration of Independence proclaimed that human

---

1   Alain de Benoist, *Kritik der Menschenrechte* (Berlin: Junge Freiheit, 2004). English edition: Alain de Benoist, *Beyond Human Rights: Defending Freedoms* (London: Arktos, 2011).

2   Ibid., 6.

3   Ibid., 7.

rights are based on "self-evident" truths.[4] Consequently, this ideology ends up being a secular world religion, unassailable in the eyes of its apologists. Anyone who criticizes this sacrosanct truth is classified as non-human. While human rights are based on the principles of tolerance and equality, they lead in practice to intolerance and total exclusion. De Benoist sees them more as declarations of war than of love.[5] Behind human rights lies not the intent of blessing humanity, but rather of restoring a clear conscience to the West from the perspective of its liberal ideology. It is probably no coincidence that human rights were loudly promulgated at the precise time when people have begun to treat each other like things and everything interpersonal has been subordinated to the exchange of goods. But the question of freedom cannot be decided morally or juridically, only politically. When criticizing this secular religion, what matters most is separating the freedom of cardinal values from the catastrophic context of universalism and subjectivity.[6]

If one considers the issue politically, one must first question the legitimacy of human rights. From the perspective of general jurisprudence, these are equated to "innate rights," or rights which are inherent to man and which he enjoys by natural law, i.e., before entering a social relationship and becoming part of a community. These can only be individual rights, posited as being present from birth. Since they are an inheritance of all mankind, they are liberated from any spatial and temporal context. Because human rights are universal and inalienable, no state can grant or abolish them. A state can only recognize them and commit itself to guaranteeing them. This is the extent of the inherent aspect of human rights. However, even though they claim an ahistorical character, and thereby pretend to be inherent in human nature from the beginning, they are not without

---

4   Ibid., 8.

5   Ibid., 9.

6   Ibid., 10–11.

history. As de Benoist meticulously explains, they are first explicitly mentioned in 1537 and are rooted in the intellectual movement of subjectivism.[7] In stark contrast with the *ius* of classical Roman law, which is directed at distributional justice and harmony within the community as well as the common good, the doctrine of human rights promoted introspection (René Descartes's famous "*cogito ergo sum*") and the individual's retreat into privacy.[8] The Christian notion of the universal brotherhood of all peoples in Christ and their equality before God is an additional precedent. Another milestone in the development of human rights is marked by the discourse of nominalism in the Middle Ages, which posited that there are only individual beings (*Wesen*) in the universe and that no other form of being (*Sein*) could be said to exist.[9] The logical conclusion of this idea is a community which is no longer greater than the sum of its parts and is reduced to an interlocking assemblage of individuals.

Finally, in the 16th century, the Salamanca School proclaimed individual reason to be the basis of natural law. In modern natural law, the individual thus became the center of the judicial universe, based on the subjective natural law of modern times instead of a divine order, and emanating entirely from human beings.[10] In Hobbes and Locke, man becomes a being constantly concerned with his own interest, one who only enters a (contractual) relationship with others if he sees an advantage in it. The social contract becomes a pact between equals, in radical contrast to the unequal covenant between God and people. Against this background, in the 17th and 18th centuries, the bourgeoisie began to use the legal means of guaranteeing private property to establish a political role commensurate with their political weight. Politics has consequently lost its status as a driving

---

7   Ibid., 12–13.

8   Ibid., 14.

9   Ibid., 19.

10   Ibid., 20–21.

force and has become a mere cause-effect relation, with the social sphere relegated to a mere consequence of the contract between individuals, and power demoted from the status of something formative to being seen as an inhumane and threatening superstructure. Interpersonal coexistence has developed into a cost-benefit relation in accordance with the logic of the market.[11]

These transformations under the aegis of individual human rights have given birth to the modern idea of "civil society." Now individuals can act freely (within certain confines) , in the private sphere, but they are excluded from political life. "Rights" are characterized by this logic of the individual subject. This leads to a threefold revolution: first, will takes the place of order, then the individual comes to occupy the central position, and then "rights" belong to this individual. The latter is equated with righteousness, understood in a moral sense. Thus, the purpose of jurisprudence is no longer to mete out equitable judgments, but to compile and enforce a code of norms and approved behavior.[12] Since the state and the law are only a means of guaranteeing individual rights, the individual subject is given unprecedented authority to legally assert himself against other individuals and can thereby bring about any number of upheavals or revolutions.

In this respect, according to de Benoist, human rights no longer have anything to do with the traditional understanding of the law, because they produce a morally contaminated law which no longer addresses being as such, but only what can be described as morally righteous action.[13] Such rights generate the dream of a united humanity, subject to universal norms and laws. This unified humanity becomes both a fact and an ideal which, once established, presents itself as something self-evident. Here, once again, we encounter the universalistic nature of human rights, which extrapolate "is" from

---

11   Ibid., 25.

12   Ibid., 26.

13   Ibid., 27–28.

"ought." The key idea behind this is that people everywhere possess the same rights because they are the same people. The aim of the ideology of human rights is therefore to subject all people to a single moral law based on the ideology of universal equality, but human rights themselves stand on shaky foundations.[14] In 1948, upwards of 150 intellectuals came together to find a common spiritual foundation for human rights, a task which proved impossible. This, de Benoist tells us, is not because there is no universal quality which all people share, but rather because the very determination of human rights is too abstract and ambiguous. Their extension to women and slaves followed only after a considerable delay. Moreover, there has never been a consensus about what constitutes human rights. For example, Article 2 of the *Declaration of the Rights of Man and of the Citizen* (1789) emphasized the right to resist oppression, while Immanuel Kant argued that one had an obligation to obey authority, even if that authority should be dictatorial.[15]

While it was still clear in 1789 that rights could not be applied retrospectively, this no longer applies to crimes against humanity. Human rights can also contradict each other, such as when positive freedoms clash with negative freedoms. In France, for example, abortion rights have existed since 1974, while the right to protect embryos from experimentation has only been active since 1994. If an embryo is not yet a human life according to this paradigm, the question arises as to why it should be protected from experiments. If the embryo is a human life, one must ask why abortion is legal. While human rights passed out of fashion during the 19th century under the influence of revolutionary doctrines and historicist ideas, they experienced a comeback with the collapse of totalitarian regimes in the 20th century and the accompanying crisis of visions for the future.[16] In addition

---

14   Ibid., 33.

15   Ibid., 36–38.

16   Ibid., 40–41.

to the question of human nature, the question of human dignity also remains problematic. Dignity bears a religious resonance, because it emanates from the human soul, by virtue of which humans may place themselves above the rest of creation. According to the founding fathers of liberalism, such as Descartes and Kant, dignity is a commodity bestowed on man *qua* his humanity. But de Benoist points out that the determination of who should or should not receive something is made by comparing character traits, which in turn refers to the ancient dignity, *dignitas*. Modern dignity sees every human as dignified simply because he is a human being. When all humans are dignified, then dignity loses its special status, and no one is dignified. The quality of particular human beings does not factor into this view. This is because the ideology of human rights treats the individual, isolated from any tradition and community, and does not recognize men and human groups in their particularity, only the abstract concept of "humanity."[17]

Since any attempt to establish human rights comes up against insurmountable difficulties, the scope of human rights is limited and lacks any real foundation. Human rights pertains to consequences without prerequisites.[18] Their consequences are all the more dramatic when one regards their relationship to the diversity of cultures. Thus, human rights' claim to universality stands in contradiction to the fact that they are a product of Enlightenment thought. They have only appeared in human cultures very late, as was the case in the European culture from which they originated.[19] In their canonical form, human rights tend towards universalism and therefore do not respect differences between cultures. Since they are universalistic, the subject they formulate is necessarily abstract. Furthermore, human rights are tied to Western culture and its traditions; hence, for example, the Jews

---

17 Ibid., 56–57.

18 Ibid., 64.

19 Ibid., 70.

were integrated into the nation during the French Revolution in order to destroy them as a separate community.

Human rights constantly conflict with human diversity, whether in the form of political systems, religious traditions, or cultural values. According to de Benoist, it is obvious that such an idea is purely Western in origin. The global generalization constituted by human rights represents an artificial intervention and "continuation of the colonial syndrome."[20] The proclamation of human rights acts as a Trojan horse aimed at destroying all collective identities, which are at once the foundation of the individual identities upon which human rights are supposed to be based.[21] One of the ultimate consequences is that human rights serve as a humanitarian scaffolding for the global expansion of the market. The West promoting them means that the old contrast between East and West is replaced by the new polarity of North and South.

The question of human rights, therefore, is not a question of succumbing to relativism, but of adopting a pluralistic attitude which does not depend on the universal validity and enforcement of human rights, but recognizes the freedom of all peoples and cultures to determine their own laws and customs and to preserve them.[22] This does not explicitly mean that approving of such practices as female circumcision or widow burning is acceptable. Changes in other cultures, argues Benoist, can be initiated only from the inside, and cannot be compelled from the outside by force of arms. The American interventions in Kosovo, Afghanistan, and Iraq testify to this.

De Benoist quotes Carl Schmitt: "Whoever invokes humanity wishes to deceive." In other words, human rights are used by powerful states as instruments of economic imperialism against weak countries.[23] Humanitarian interventions do not solve problems, but

---

20 Ibid., 73.

21 Ibid., 80.

22 Ibid., 94–95.

23 Ibid., 112.

only multiply them by waging war in the name of an absolute good, thereby demonizing the opponent.[24] A further problem of human rights lies in the fact that, from their very beginnings, they have tended towards an anti-political worldview. In this worldview, the question as to what extent the community can demand certain duties from the individual is intentionally omitted. Already during the French Revolution, the problem of reconciling the people and civil rights was overwhelming. At that time, Rousseau proclaimed the primacy of the citizen over the collective and established the prerogative of the nation-state. Karl Marx, in turn, recognized that abstract human rights were mainly a privilege of the ruling class, since it was this group which determined the limits of such rights.[25] Ultimately, human rights debase the individual to nullity since, through them, he loses the qualities that enable others to treat him as their equal.[26] By robbing the individual of all concrete characteristics, such as belonging to particular groups like national and religious communities (i.e., political characteristics), these "rights" reduce man to an isolated individual.

Communitarians take a different approach, arguing that the rights of the individual remains a pure illusion as long as no general social good exists. They criticize liberalism for ignoring the collective dimension of human life that is necessary for both personal development and the definition of a good life. When it comes to seeking a basis for freedom, human rights do not suffice, given that they act as sledgehammer for the enforcement of globalization. Alain de Benoist proposes that they can be countered by drawing on the ancient concept of freedom, the Christian Imperium of the Middle Ages, civic republicanism, and finally, communitarianism.[27]

---

24 Ibid., 113.

25 Ibid., 118–120.

26 Ibid., 136.

27 Ibid., 153.

Carl Schmitt: The Concept of the Political and the *Nomos* of the Earth

C ARL SCHMITT, born in Plettenberg in 1888, was a constitutional jurist, political philosopher, and representative of the Conservative Revolution, ranking among the most famous figures of this intellectual movement. His most important writings for the New Right include *The Concept of the Political* (1932), *The Great Space Order of International Law with a Prohibition on Intervention for Spatially Foreign Powers: A Contribution to the Concept of Reich in International Law* (1939),[1] *Land and Sea: A World-Historical Meditation* (1942), and *The Nomos of the Earth in the International Law of Jus Publicum Europaeum* (1950).

In his work *The Concept of the Political*, Carl Schmitt presents his understanding of politics as inherently antagonistic. According to Schmitt, the defining political distinction to which actions and motives can be traced is the distinction between friend and foe.[2] The purpose of this distinction is to determine a political polarity in the sense of a maximum possible antithesis. The determination of an enemy is not immediately an evaluation of them as being morally reprehensible or evil. Nor does it mean that this enemy must be fought to the point of physical extinction. Schmitt expressly states that even trade and cooperation with the enemy might be useful at times. The political enemy is simply the other, a stranger with whom conflicts

---

1 In German: *Völkerrechtliche Großraumordnung mit Interventionsverbot für raumfremde Mächte: Ein Beitrag zum Reichsbegriff im Völkerrecht.*

2 Carl Schmitt, *Der Begriff des Politischen*, 25.

are also possible in extreme cases, whenever previously established norms or a neutral arbitrator between the two parties fail to ameliorate their disagreement.[3] In cases when the friend-foe dichotomy does not manifest itself on the level of external politics, but predominates in domestic politics, then the Political becomes synonymous with party politics. The antagonism then manifests itself in the distribution of sinecures and the filling of posts instead of wars. In this context, the demand for the depoliticization of life does not mean an end to the Political, but only an end to party politics. The development towards the party-political friend-foe dichotomy can only take place if the unity of the state is weakened. If the primacy of domestic policy predominates, then, Schmitt insists, one can no longer speak of a war between organised ethnicities, but only of the conflict between citizens internally, i.e., civil war.[4]

What is important about Schmitt's definition of the Political is that it has a purely descriptive function. Having established this concept, Carl Schmitt does not desire to make the case for either a militaristic position or a pacifist one; he does not promote successful revolution (in the communist sense) or victorious war (in the fascist/ National-Socialist sense) as social ideals. In contrast to the often incorrectly reproduced quote from Carl von Clausewitz that war is "the continuation of politics by other means," Schmitt attributes to war its own independent laws and principles. The only thing it presupposes on the part of politics is the identification and determination of the enemy.[5] War, in Schmitt's understanding, is therefore neither the purpose nor the content of politics, but rather an ever-present possibility which determines human action and thinking, thereby effecting a specific political behaviour. The essence of the Political is not that certain peoples live in eternal enmity, or that neutrality becomes

---

3   Ibid., 26.

4   Ibid., 30.

5   Ibid., 32.

impossible in the event of war. Rather, war is a state of emergency in which the extreme consequence of classification between friend and foe shows itself. Only through this most extreme possibility do people's lives gain their specific political tension. In this sense, Carl Schmitt also opposes the liberalist-pacifist idea of a world without war. A completely pacified world in which the possibility of war and the friend-foe relationship no longer exist, Schmitt argues, would be a world without politics.

In response to the question as to whether politics is the driving force behind wars instead of religion, the economy, or morality, Schmitt clearly favors the political side. If moral, economic, or religious differences were to be exacerbated to the point of causing a friend-foe dynamic, then they would no longer be purely moral, economic, or religious, but would become political. The critical question which always resurfaces is whether the friend-foe antagonism is strong enough to exist as a real possibility, rather than the question of whether human motives are strong enough to effect it.[6] In this sense, Schmitt also strongly pronounces himself against the idea of waging a "war to end all wars" to establish a world peace that encompasses all peoples, because such wars are inevitably inhuman and cruel, since they go beyond the Political. In wars such as these, the enemy inevitably gets demonized and dehumanized, becoming something that is not only to be opposed, but ultimately to be destroyed.[7] In Schmitt's view, broadcasting anti-war propaganda and mobilizing the general public for a total war against the enemy targeted for total destruction under the pretext of preventing another war is nothing but deception. This is because war has no normativity. Rather, it possesses an existential quality, and can only be waged against a real enemy, without any reference to ideals. A war that is not waged in response to an existential threat to the nation, according to Schmitt,

---

6   Ibid., 33.

7   Ibid., 35.

simply cannot be justified.[8] As Schmitt sees it, the decision as to whether an emergency exists, and who the foe is, must belong to the people themselves, and must not be hampered by any judicial norms or non-governmental third parties. The political essence of a people consists precisely in the power of decision-making during an emergency. If the people has lost the ability and will to decide between friend and foe, they cease to exist politically. Moreover, if a nation can no longer decide for itself who are its friends and foes, this power is eventually captured by a foreign force, which subordinates this indecisive entity to its own political system.[9] If a people desires to assert itself, it must do so in the political sphere. Simply denying the friend-foe dichotomy does not lead to the end of the Political. A people and nation may cease to exist if they lose their will to determine who is friend and who is foe, but the Political itself never disappears.[10]

With regard to the geopolitical thought of the New Right, the theory of a multipolar world, as well as the discourse which stems from the German idea of "Great Space" (*Großraum*) and sees civilization as a political entity beyond the state, Schmitt's most relevant works are *The Großraum Order of International Law, Land and Sea*, and *Nomos of the Earth*. In these books, Schmitt conceptualizes an early blueprint of a multipolar world order made up of "Great Spaces," challenging the idea of a liberal, unipolar world order. In his postulation of a "Great Space Order" (*Großraumordnung*) of international law — noteworthily published in 1939 — Carl Schmitt defines a Great Space as that which combines a politically awakened people, a political idea, and a Great Space to be governed by that idea and protected from foreign interventions.[11] Schmitt refers to the Monroe Doctrine as a model, but not to the liberal-imperialist form of the doctrine that

---

8   Ibid., 46.

9   Ibid., 47.

10   Ibid., 50.

11   Carl Schmitt, *Völkerrechtliche Großraumordnung mit Interventionsverbot für raumfremde Mächte: Ein Beitrag zum Reichsbegriff im Völkerrecht*, 30.

had already spanned across Europe and other broad swathes of the world by the 1920s and 1930s; instead, his reference is to the notion of a Great Space which can interdict the influence of alien powers. This is even more important today, (nearly a century after Schmitt's initial formuations, since Western democracies have found themselves in a strikingly similar position to that of the Holy Alliance after the Napoleonic Wars: instead of a monarchic-dynastic principle of legitimacy, all current non-liberal and non-Western powers are being confronted by the hegemony of liberal-democratic capitalism, which regards any system out of step with its own as illegitimate. Following the presidential tenure of Theodore Roosevelt (1858–1919), the Monroe Doctrine transformed into a justification of capitalist imperialism.[12] Its first major manifestation was America's intervention in the First World War, followed by America's move to destabilize and topple the governments of a whole host of South American nations. According to Schmitt, this shift came about when what was initially a doctrine concerned with a proscribed geographical zone ended up projected onto a global, universal scale. This transforms the "healthy core of a large-scale international legal principle of non-intervention into an imperialist, pan-interventionist world ideology that interferes in everything under humanitarian pretexts."[13] It is important to note that Schmitt divides the Great Space into individual realms and does not equate any one state with the entire Great Space.[14] By "realm" (*Reich*), Schmitt explicitly does not mean the nation-state, but rather he sees in the people, and the realm constituted by one or more peoples, a "Great Space Order" that goes beyond and overcomes the nation-state. With reference to Gottfried Neeße, he differentiates between the state as an organizational form and the people as an

---

12   Ibid., 31.

13   Ibid., 33.

14   Ibid., 49.

organism. Schmitt assumes that a realm can also include several peoples, because not every nation can create its own realm.

In order to counter liberal universalism, Schmitt regards the state as an important element of Great Space Order which must constantly set its boundaries. Thus, besides nationality and ethnic origin, the Great Space Order must also be demarcated territorially.[15] According to Schmitt, the guarantor against the non-intervention of foreign powers is always the people which sees itself as the political custodian of the Great Space.[16] Four different forms of legal relationships result from this relation of Great Spaces: (1) economic cooperation, (2) collaboration between the leading Great Spaces, (3) inter-ethnic relationships, and (4) negotiations relating to non-intervention or non-interference between the peoples of the respective Great Spaces.[17] In pursuing his intentions to limit the possibilities of war, as well as to establish a lasting peace, Schmitt also calls for a drawing of peace lines which would enable the emergence of war-free spaces and provide the means for resolving conflicts beyond this line without escalating into major armed conflicts between the Great Spaces.[18]

In *Land and Sea*, Carl Schmitt provides a historico-philosophical basis for his critique of the liberal world order, written in the form of a story to his daughter Anima. In this story, he relates human history as a struggle between sea and land powers. Capitalism, liberal democracy, and human rights are trappings of the sea powers, while any bulwarks of conservative order are identified with land powers.[19] This eternal conflict is epitomized by the struggle between two biblical monsters: Leviathan (often depicted as sea serpent or great whale) and Behemoth (described as a bull, elephant, or hippopotamus). Schmitt sees a rebellion against human nature in the the buccaneers

---

15 Ibid., 59.

16 Ibid., 61.

17 Ibid., 62.

18 Ibid., 71.

19 Carl Schmitt, *Land und Meer*, 16.

and rovers of the sea (*Seeschäumern*) who emerged from modern England, for man is originally a land being.

Combining these approaches, Schmitt calls for a new division of the world into Great Spaces. The central work in which he does so is *Nomos of the Earth*. Schmitt recognizes in the concept of *Nomos* (derived from the classical Greek *nemein* (νέμειν) — "to allot what is due") the direct embodiment of the political and social order of a people in its spatially visible form.[20] In this arrangement, there will not be one single universe, but instead a pluriverse of different states — a "Great Space Order."[21]

In this new division of the planet, he perceives the continuum of history, and seeks a means of escaping that history's "end."[22] In the context of his five introductory corollaries to the *Nomos of the Earth*, Schmitt also addresses the tradition of European international law as it existed before modernity. Here, he underlines the importance of the *katekhon* (τὸ κατέχον) ("that which withholds"), as seen in the figure of the emperor, who acts as "restrainer" against the Antichrist. He finds it remarkable that the Christian *Imperium* was aware of its temporal limitations, and foresaw its apocalyptic conclusion while nonetheless remaining a historical power.[23] By contrast, Schmitt regards European universalism and the global expansion of its judicial framework as a tragedy that grew out of the comparatively local and genuinely European Middle Ages. According to Schmitt, this tragedy was rooted in the universalization of European international law in the wake of the colonial partition of Africa, beginning with the occupation of the Congo by neutral Belgium.[24] This land grab demonstrated, for the first time, that Europe had lost the power to maintain its own Space Structure (*Raumstruktur*) and the ability to prevent

---

20 Ibid., 39.

21 Ibid., 216.

22 Ibid., 48.

23 Ibid., 29.

24 Ibid., 198.

war. Through this event, Europeans lost their awareness of this Space Structure; from that point on, their conception of law ceased to be European and instead became universalistic. Henceforth, it became sufficient to display the "right attitude" or "mindset" in order to be included in the global system.[25]

In order to lift Europe and its peoples once more up into the sphere of the Political, Schmitt advocates not only a multipolar world and a pluriverse of political ideas and Great Spaces, but also for a rehabilitation of the Political, of the friend-foe dichotomy, and understanding legitimate war. All of these ideas, couched in the context of the historic antagonism between sea and land powers, have exerted a great influence on the New Right, one that can be observed throughout the movement's intellectual history concerning metapolitics and geopolitics.

---

25 Ibid., 205–206.

The Conservative Revolution
and Oswald Spengler

WHEN ONE looks for the intellectual pioneers of the New Right, the thinkers of the German Conservative Revolution are the first to come to mind. The concept of Conservative Revolution counts among the most dazzling, but also the most confusing, terms in intellectual history. What sounds like a contradiction (between the word "conservative," denoting a preservation of what there already is, and the word "revolution," primarily understood as total overthrow of the latter) is, upon closer examination, a semantic repetition, as the word revolution in this context denotes its original 15th-century Latin sense, "to roll back." Edgar Julius Jung (1894–1934), who is considered one of the most important German Conservative Revolutionaries, defined it in the following way: "We call 'Conservative' the Revolution that reinstates elementary laws and values, without which man loses his connection to nature and God, and cannot establish true order."[1]

Consequently, the Conservative Revolution was directed against the liberal-capitalist order which emerged from modernity. Thus, its goal — in the sense of Friedrich Nietzsche's heroic realism — was first to eliminate the existing order so as to then establish an order worth preserving. The critical prerequisite for this will towards overcoming the modern world is understanding the modern, progress-worshiping, mechanized mass-society as a society in crisis. Thus, René

---

1   Edgar Julius Jung, *Deutschland und die Konservative Revolution* (1932).

Guénon, a French representative of Traditionalism that influenced the Conservative Revolution, accused modernist society of being a strict negation of Tradition, i.e., a society which has ceased to recognize transcendent truths. The problem of modern society lies in its materialism and its negation of spirituality.[2]

The Conservative Revolution was by no means limited to Germany; it found supporters all over Europe, as well as in Russia and the United States, although it managed to become a dominant intellectual current only in the Weimar Republic.[3] Among its most prominent representatives are the Germans Edgar Julius Jung, Carl Schmitt, and Oswald Spengler, the Russians Fyodor Dostoyevsky and Konstantin Aksakov, the Frenchmen George Sorel, Maurice Barrès, and René Guénon, the Italians Vilfredo Pareto and Julius Evola, the Spaniard Miguel de Unamnuo, the Briton Keith Chesterton, and the American James Burnham.[4] In the Germanophone space, the Conservative Revolution can be divided into five different currents:

1) The "Völkisch Movement" [*Völkische Bewegung*] (with a central emphasis on a biologically driven national idea (*Volksgedanke*), and the idea of an ethnic community (*Volksgemeinschaft*);

2) The "Young Conservatives" [*Jungkonservativen*] (oriented towards the idea of Empire — *Reich, Imperium*), including Oswald Spengler, Edgar Julius Jung, and Arthur Moeller van den Bruck);

3) The "National Revolutionaries" [*Nationalrevolutionäre*] (revolutionary overcoming of the state, the experience of the first World War, and combat experience within the Freikorps, heroic realism, orientation towards the East), e.g., Ernst Jünger, Ernst Niekisch;

---

2   René Guénon, *The Crisis of the Modern World* (Ghent: Sophia Perennis, 2001), 108.

3   Karlheinz Weißmann, *Die Konservative Revolution in Europa. Berliner Schriften zur Ideologienkunde* 3 (Verein für Staatspolitik, 2013), 7.

4   Tomislav Sunic, *Against Democracy and Equality: The European New Right* (London: Arktos, 2012), 81.

4) The "Leaguists" [*Bündischen*] (the life reform movement, cultivation of customs and traditions, emphasis on the education and upbringing of the youth);

5) The "rural people's movement" (the peasant uprising against the authorities of Schleswig-Holstein).

Oswald Spengler counts among the most influential thinkers of the Conservative Revolution with his work *The Decline of the West* (*Der Untergand des Abendlandes*). Published in two volumes (the first in 1917 during the First World War in anticipation of a German victory, the second in 1922), this work sees itself as a comprehensive historical morphology — and as a still incomplete one, despite being over 1,000 pages in length. In this work, Spengler sought to identify the general laws of history by comparing the European North and American West with seven other high cultures, tracing patterns of cultural rise and fall. Spengler decisively rejected the idea of a single humanity,[5] describing in his work the inevitable end of Western culture and its withering into an ossified form (*Erstarrung*). In his view, cultures are like living organisms that have a life cycle moving through birth, youth, old age, and death. For the interpreter of history, the growth of cultures is of "sublime futility," yet cannot be stopped by man. What is of interest here is the idea that progress does not exist, and that cultures, like individuals, are mortal. For Spengler, every culture goes through different "seasons." While it may reach its mature phase during "Summer" or "Autumn," it freezes to a husk during "Winter" and sees its demise in the end phase as "civilization." The course of this process can vary by nation, geographic area, and era.

As a rule of thumb, however, it is said that every culture reaches its phase of decline after about 1,000 years. Thus, according to Spengler, European culture was reborn in the 9th century and entered the period of its cultural decline in the 19th century. However,

---

5   Ibid., 92.

Spengler maintains that what leads to the birth of a culture remains a mystery. Since reaching its expiration phase, European "Civilization" has been endangered by an advanced form of social, political, and cultural decline. This final phase was reached in the wake of the Industrial Revolution, when Europe abandoned its culture and entered the phase of civilization. Moreover, this phase is characterized by the rule of a plutocracy and an ideology of economism. All aspects of life are placed in a relation to the economy. Because everyone wants more and more, there is a societal hunger for change.[6] Spengler regards this inevitable downfall of Western culture not as a catastrophe, such as a plane crash, but as a slow and steady decline which has already been observed in other cultures.

Spengler sees civilization as the end phase of culture, following on from the negative connotations of the term as it is used in the German language. This condition is marked by a variety of symptoms of decay. Spengler mentions materialism and irreligiousness, loss of history, a collapse of morals, the disappearance of art, an entertainment industry running by the credo of "bread and circuses," the artificially induced torpor of all areas of life, the rise of formless violence, and imperialism with its wars and struggles-to-the-death between civilizations. Spengler, whose philosophy of history assumed that people gather around strong leaders in times of chaos, saw the future of the West in Caesarism, which he understood as the rule of a charismatic leader. However, to deduce in this sense any support for National Socialism would be erroneous, for Spengler rejected Hitler and his party, but he did see in Mussolini an embodiment of the coming Caesar, presaging the end times. It is no coincidence that Spengler believed that the transition from democracy to mob rule (in the sense of the masses) occurs when the tyranny of the few is replaced by the tyranny of the majority. It is precisely this appearance of the modern masses as political actors which the representatives

---

6   Ibid., 93.

of Conservative Revolution condemned as an expression of modern politics.[7]

Thus, the West is heading towards its demise, but what is to be done in this situation? Oswald Spengler recommends that Europeans abandon their narrow view so that they can understand the temporality of their perspective and develop different political attitudes. For how would Parsifal and Prometheus be applicable to the average Japanese? He also reminds his reader that Bacon and Kant would not attach much importance to modern Chinese and Arabs, and that Western European culture is precisely not universal, even if Europeans have imagined it to be so.[8] As the Spenglerian Heinrich Scholz ascertained, there could not be a single path of development if history were a singular unity rather than a polycentric plurality. What was revolutionary in Spengler's conception of history was his view that modernity has entailed a loss of understanding of the fact that history is divided into distinct, autonomous, cyclical units. Moreover, precisely because Europe finds itself in its demise, it is unfit to serve as a role model for other cultures.[9]

Against the reactions of many of his contemporaries alleging that he was only disseminating a demoralizing pessimism, Spengler responded as follows: because man cannot resist his fate, he must submit to it. Spengler did not foresee a bright future within the liberal or socialist matrix of progress.[10] The only place where he could discern progress was in the minds of the progress-mongers. He repeatedly rejected the designation of pessimist applied to him because, in his eyes, the term could only be applied to those who had relinquished their duties. But, according to Spengler, the problem lies in the fact

---

7   Ibid., 94.

8   Ibid.

9   Ibid., 95.

10 Ibid., 96.

that there are many urgent matters, for which both men and time are lacking.[11]

Throughout its existence, the Conservative Revolution's representatives were always in a tense relationship with National Socialism. While some took the path of resistance against National Socialism and ended up in a concentration camp (Ernst Niekisch) or murdered (Edgar Julius Jung), others reluctantly collaborated (temporarily) with the regime (Martin Heidegger, Carl Schmitt). Both the Conservative Revolution's critique of democracy and the effectiveness of its propaganda can be understood through the example of Edgar Julius Jung's work *The Rule of the Inferior: Its Disintegration and Removal Through a New Reich* (*Die Herrschaft Der Minderwertigen — Ihr Zerfall und ihre Abloesung durch ein neues Reich*). Jung's *dictum* states that, much like his contemporary Robert Michels claimed, democracy tends towards oligarchy, which then no longer represents a form of government in which the best rules, but rather one ruled by those who are best at scheming: the corrupt and well-connected. Jung believed that, by phasing out the rule of the inferior, a holistic *Imperium* (or *Reich*) with a corporative structure would take its place, in which individualism would be superseded by the rule of personalities. Due to its popularity, this slogan was co-opted by the National Socialists, much in the same way as the term "Third Reich" [*Drittes Reich*] was appropriated from Arthur Moeller van den Bruck and used to describe the National-Socialist state (even as it remained a nation-state, tied only superficially to the imperial idea [*Reichsidee*]).

In conclusion, how can the Conservative Revolution be integrated into the thought of the New Right? In Alexander Dugin's assessment, the Conservative Revolution was the first attempt to find a way out of modernity, beyond liberalism, communism, and fascism. The Conservative Revolutionaries were engaged on three frontlines:

----

11   Ibid., 97.

against liberalism, against fascism and the Third Position (especially against attempts to appropriate the intellectual concepts articulated by Conservative Revolutionaries), and against communism. But the circumstances in the 21st century are much clearer: liberalism is the main and single enemy of all free peoples.[12] Today, it is up to the New Right and proponents of Dugin's Fourth Political Theory to embrace the Conservative-Revolutionary legacy and seek a way out of postmodernity.

---

12 Alexander Dugin, *The Rise of the Fourth Political Theory [The Fourth Political Theory Vol. II]* (London: Arktos, 2017), 82–82.

The Fourth Political Theory

THE BOOK *The Fourth Political Theory* [Четвёртая политическая теория], often abbreviated to "4PT," serves as the political manifesto of the Russian philosopher, sociologist, and geopolitical thinker Alexander Dugin. Born on January 7, 1962 in Moscow to an officer in Soviet military intelligence and a doctor, Dugin engaged early on with the Traditionalism of René Guénon and Julius Evola. Initially a student at the Moscow Aviation Institute, he lost his place at university due to his associations with the Moscow metaphysical underground and, more immediately, his performances of "mystical anti-Soviet songs."[1] Dugin gained recognition in the Traditionalist underground for his Russian-language translation of Julius Evola's early book *Pagan Imperialism*. His expulsion from the Aviation Institute left him with few means of sustenance, and he spent a brief stint as a street sweeper. After traveling to Europe, making the acquaintances of Jean Thiriart and Alain de Benoist, and familiarizing himself with their Francophone publications, Dugin established the Russian-language journal *Elements* [Элементы] and initiated an intimate collaboration with the Moscow-based magazine *Day* [День]. After the collapse of the USSR, Dugin's first involvement with a political party was when he joined the newly formed Communist Party of the Russian Federation (CPRF)

---

1   Jafe Arnold, "Mysteries of Eurasia: The Esoteric Sources of Alexander Dugin and the Yuzhinsky Circle," MA thesis (Amsterdam: Center for the History of Hermetic Philosophy and Related Currents, Department of Religious Studies, Faculty of Humanities, University of Amsterdam, 2019).

[Коммунистическая Партия Российской Федерации (КПРФ)], helmed by Gennady Andreyevich Zyuganov, in which he sought to instill a markedly national-revolutionary program. When this failed, he went on to found a chimerical entity that was at once a neo-avant-garde art project and a political program based entirely on radical, anti-liberal ideas: the National Bolshevik Party (NBP) [Национал-большевистская партия (НБП)]. Together with the *poète-épateur* Eduard Limonov and the punk musician Yegor Letov, he forged young and wild cadre, for whom Boris Yeltsin's 1993 putsch against the Russian Parliament and tank shelling of the parliamentary White House became a formative experience.

While in contact with Alain de Benoist, Dugin began to disseminate the ideas of the Conservative Revolution and the New Right to wider audiences in Russia by means of his publishing house, Arktogeia, and his numerous appearances on Russian television. In doing so, he has exerted significant influence on Putin's regime, particularly on matters of geopolitics. One major event in this regard was the publication of his 1997 geopolitical primer, *Foundations of Geopolitics* (Основы геополитики), which was adopted as a textbook for the Russian General Staff.[2] After the end of his National Bolshevik phase in 1998, Dugin dedicated himself increasingly to the idea of Eurasia as inspired by the Eurasianist school of thought from the 1920s-30s, developing it under the influence of the Conservative Revolution and the New Right. These efforts led to the foundation of the Eurasia Party, which was converted into the Eurasian Movement after suffering parliamentary electoral failure. The International Eurasian Movement remains active to this day.

In 2010, Dugin became a professor in the sociology of international relations at the renowned Lomonosov Moscow State University. In his interviews with the international press and in his

---

2   Dugin's Foundations of Geopolitics has been partially translated into German under the title Konflikte der Zukunft ("Conflicts of the Future"), published in 2015.

public appearances, Dugin tends towards radical and decisive statements, a factor that makes him a highly controversial figure not only in the eyes of the Western media, but also in the sphere of Russian politics. "Putin's brain," "Putin's Rasputin," and "fascist" are only some of the labels that have been applied to him, and show that his influence on Russian politics ranges in the estimation of his critics from comprehensive to marginal. An illustrative example of this is a statement which he gave in a 2014 interview which resulted in outrage and, ultimately, his ousting from Moscow State University. In the interview, Dugin responded to the murder of several Russians by Ukrainian ultranationalists with a call for vengeance and the physical destruction of the Ukrainian elite.

Despite his numerous globalist detractors, Dugin's ideas have found appeal all over the world: he has participated in conferences not only in Russia, but also in the Middle East, Turkey, and Iran. He also maintains close connections with Latin America — for example, in Brazil with Flavia Virginia, who leads the Centre for Multipolarity Studies, dedicated to the study of the Fourth Political Theory, as well as the *Nova Resistência* movement (for whom Dugin is a major ideological godfather). His ideas have also found a vigorous reception in the United States and Canada, partly owing to the philosopher Michael Millerman, while in the People's Republic of China, Dugin has held a visiting professor position at Fudan University, in Shanghai. In Europe, the publishing house Arktos has been his sole English-language publisher, while numerous English translations of selected texts have also been published online by the Eurasianist Internet Archive.[3]

Dugin's *Fourth Political Theory* first appeared in Russian in 2008, before receiving its English-language publication in 2012. Conceptualized in collaboration with Alain de Benoist, this text does not postulate a finalized theory, but instead lays the groundwork for

---

3   Eurasianist Internet Archive [eurasianist-archive.com].

an open concept that systematically condenses many ideas of the New Right. The background of the Fourth Political Theory is its view of the 20th century as a century of ideologies. All ideologies which became influential in that century, Dugin asserts, were products of modernity. Nowadays, we have experienced a crisis of ideologies, or even the end of ideologies in general.[4] The three primary ideologies of the 20th century, Dugin tells us, are first liberalism (both in its left and right form), then communism (to include its Marxist, socialist, and social-democratic variants), and finally fascism (under which heading he also includes National Socialism and other variations of Third Position politics). The drama of the past century was centered on the fight between these three ideologies.

The first political theory, liberalism, has been the most successful ideology, given that it has vanquished its rivals. This victory entitled liberalism to regard itself as the true successor to the Enlightenment. Liberalism found itself challenged by the second political theory, communism, which articulated itself as a critical response to the bourgeois-capitalist system. Fascism then emerged as the third political theory, simultaneously combatting both preceding ideologies before collapsing under the strain of its own suicidal geopolitics. With fascism out of the way, the path was clear for the fight between liberalism and communism, the victor of which was to be recognized as the true heir of modernity. This conflict found expression in the bipolar world order of the Cold War and concluded in the victory of liberalism in 1991.[5]

However, Dugin claims, the paradox of this victorious liberalism is that as soon as it emerged unchallenged at the end of the 20th century, it reached an apparent end. Unlike communism and fascism, which each had to struggle for their very survival before succumbing,

---

4   Dugin's *Foundations of Geopolitics* has been partially translated into German under the title *Konflikte der Zukunft* ("Conflicts of the Future"), published in 2015.

5   *Eurasianist Internet Archive* [eurasianist-archive.com].

liberalism was from the beginning an idea which sought to create a monopoly for itself as the sole representative of modernity. Although liberalism presents itself as less dogmatic than Marxism, it is no less philosophical or refined than its rival. While the other ideologies still existed, liberalism strengthened itself as a depository of ideas, viewpoints, and projects, continually developing its intellectual concepts, as is typical for a historical subject. While the subject of communism was a collective social class, fascism focused on the state, and National Socialism centered itself on the race; the subject of liberalism, however, is the notional "individual." What defines this individual is its liberation from any conceivable form of collective identity. In the struggle for the true legacy of modernity, every nation and society had a choice between its three main ideological variants. But, with the victory of liberalism, the individual became the real subject of modern development. This victory enabled the phenomenon of globalization and established the model for the post-industrial society. Since the victory of liberalism, being an "individual" has ceased to be a free choice, and instead has become compulsory. As part of liberalism's emerging hegemony, humanity, now consisting entirely of individuals, is a universal, global concept. This idea has given birth to the project of world government and globalism. New technological developments have made people independent from modern class structures and enabled the emergence of a post-industrial society. The values of rationalism, scientism, and positivism have been recognized and critiqued as a disguised form of repression. At the same time, any impediments to such developments — namely, reason, morality, and identity — have been liquidated in the name of the individual's "freedom." All of these developments were the conditions for entry into post-modernity.[6]

At this point, liberalism ceases to be the first political theory and becomes the only possible post-political praxis. With the advent

---

6   Alexander Dugin, *The Fourth Political Theory* (London: Arktos, 2012), 15.

of Francis Fukuyama's "End of History," the economy in the form of international capital has come to replace politics, states, and nations, which have been dissolved in the melting pot of globalization. Liberalism is no longer a political dimension in which one still has a free choice, but has become a historically determined fate. The economy has become the fate of the people. Thus, the beginning of the 21st century coincides with the end of ideology, or rather the end of all three ideologies of modernity. Whereas the third political theory fFascism) was destroyed in its youth, and the second political theory (communism) died in old age, the first political theory (liberalism) was reborn as something else in the form of post-liberalism and the global market society. Against this background, it is logical that the political theories of modernity are no longer able to explain present events or react to new global challenges.[7]

In the postmodern era, machines and technology threaten to replace everything. Politics has been reduced to the administration of the *status quo*. Technocrats have taken the place of politicians, in order to manage everything as effectively as possible. With this development, one must always keep in mind that when liberals speak of the end of all ideologies, they do not cease believing in their own ideology; instead, they seek to deny everyone else the right to an ideology of their own. Moreover, as presented above, liberalism itself has undergone a transformation: instead of articulating itself at the level of the subject, a position it held in modernity, it turns the subject into an object in postmodernity. This also underlies the liberal will to completely replace reality through virtuality.

This is where the Fourth Political Theory (4PT) comes into play. It comes into conflict with this reality and rejects postmodernity in its essence. The 4PT is set against postmodernity, the post-industrial society, liberal thought implemented in praxis, globalization, and its

---

7   Ibid., 15–17.

technological and logistical principles.[8] It proposes two alternatives: not the decision between Left and Right, but between complicity with postmodern liberalism or resistance against it. One either positions himself in the global center, or he becomes part of the periphery. In this way, the 4PT challenges liberalism in its new form. With its victory, liberalism acquired the right to forge the end of history in accordance with its own ideas. Theoretically, this end of history could also have been a National-Socialist planetary Reich, or global communism. Nonetheless, it was the first political theory which emerged as the victor of modernity, and Dugin suggests that the battle for postmodernity has only just begun.

In postmodernity, the dictatorship of ideas has been replaced by the dictatorship of things. Just as the second and third political theories attempted to tame modernity in their struggle against liberalism, one must nowadays exploit the loopholes of postmodernity. For Dugin, liberalism's victory has created the conditions for its own disappearance. One need only find chinks in this global system's armor in order to hack in and start doing damage. Thus, the 4PT must draw its "dark inspiration" from postmodernity and the liquidation of the Enlightenment, the advent of the society of simulacra. Just as Marx could only take up the struggle against capitalism after having brilliantly understood its structures, one must learn the structures of postmodernity today; this is the only way to fight it. Postmodernity should not be accepted as fate, but rather as an invitation for struggle.[9] Upon looking back at the failures of the second and third political theories, it is important to keep in mind that their defeat at the hands of liberalism is proof of their non-belonging to the modern paradigm. Their failure can be attributed an excess of traditionality somehow present within them, despite their modern trappings.

---

8   Ibid., 18.

9   Ibid., 19.

The radical rejection of postmodernity by the 4PT begins in the realm of religion. As an integral part of Tradition, religion is a necessary pillar of resistance against modernity. Postmodernity, unlike modernity, is not hostile towards religion, but rather indifferent, an attitude which Dugin finds even more abhorrent. Dugin sees in postmodernity the kingdom of the Antichrist from the Christian perspective, the *Kali-Yuga* [कलियुग] in the Hindu conception, the *Dajjāl* [دجّال] from an Islamic perspective, and the *Erev Rav* [עֵרֶב רַב] of messianic Judaism. For the contemporary world, postmodernity is experienced precisely as the Apocalypse.[10] While modernity was characterized by an aggressive atheism, the proponents of the 4PT must ignore anyone who speaks of the death of God as though they were mad. What remains is to examine the mechanisms of modernity and postmodernity, utilizing what is useful and discarding what is not in a bid to overcome them.

What useful insights can be drawn from a critical examination of communism from the Right and of fascism from the Left? In the case of communism, what is most useful is its critique of capitalism and bourgeois society. In fascism, ethnocentrism serves as a positive element, even if ethnocentrism was never its focal point. By "ethnocentrism," Dugin means a positive attitude towards one's own people, and the will to defend them against liberal globalization. Even in liberalism, Dugin finds a positive feature in the notions of freedom "to" and freedom "from." By this, however, he does not explicitly mean freedom for the individual, but freedom for human groups: the people and civilization. One must escape from the prison of the individual and rediscover the freedom of peoples before one can understand the real meaning of freedom. Hence, the 4PT views liberalism and the philosophy of the "Open Society" as propounded by Karl Popper as its chief enemies. The 4PT proclaims that every form of human identity is acceptable except for the individual. Liberalism must be

---

10   Ibid., 20–21.

defeated and destroyed, so that the individual can be pushed off his pedestal.

Proceeding from this deconstruction, Dugin declares Martin Heidegger's concept of *Dasein* ("There-Being") to be the subject of the 4PT, under which he understands *Being* (*Sein*) to be tied to a certain place and, by extension, a people.[11] As is also the case with the ethnopluralism of the New Right, Dugin diverges with Martin Heidegger on this point; he does not recognize only one *Dasein*, but acknowledges a plurality of *Daseins* which must be preserved by the peoples belonging to them. Geopolitically, it is necessary to leave the nation-state behind us, since it is no longer capable of defending peoples against globalization. In its place, the concept of "civilizations" should take precedence. Dugin concept of "civilizations" is analogous to Schmitt's *Great Space* (*Grossraum*), an entity that unites peoples along common cultural, historical, and linguistic lines, and whose scale reinforces them in the event that the United States should attempt to embargo them. Following Samuel P. Huntington's *Clash of Civilizations*, Dugin thus takes up the idea that civilizations are the future subjects of world politics. However, while Huntington is critical of the coming multipolar world and the resulting decline of hegemonic US power, even assuming a necessary conflict (especially with Islam and China), Dugin regards this conflict not as an eventuality, but merely as a possibility. The multipolar world which he proposes as an alternative to the unipolar world should reject the "End of History" and the universalism of Western civilization. Instead of the "one world" of western civilization, there should be many worlds.

Here, Dugin takes pains not to assume different interpretations of "the world," but rather seeks to postulate a number of parallel worlds existing on the same planet, represented by different civilizations. In this scheme, Dugin identifies the following civilizations: Western civilization (consisting of a continental European and a

---

11   Ibid., 52.

North-American Atlantic Great Space), Eurasian civilization (including not only Slavs and the Orthodox of the Russian world, but also other ethnic groups, such as the Islamic, Caucasian, and Siberian peoples of the region), Islamic civilization (consisting of an Arab Great Space, a continental Islamic Great Space — Iran, Afghanistan, and Pakistan — and an Islamic Great Space in the Pacific), Chinese civilization, Japanese civilization, Indian civilization, a potential Latin-American Civilization, Buddhist civilization, and a possible African civilization. The 4PT thus represents a revolutionary ideology, which desires to overcome postmodernism and everything that defines it. For Europeans, this ideology presents the prospects of overcoming American hegemony. Thus, Dugin's Fourth Political Theory is, in the truest sense, a pluralistic idea that summons all of the world's civilizations to resist globalization.

Who Are the People? Ethnosociology as Key to Understanding Modernity

ONE OF the great merits of Alexander Dugin as a professor of sociology is, on the one hand, having made this field fertile for the New Right and, on the other hand, having rediscovered the discipline of ethnosociology. There is a consciously created confusion in the West about the terms "tribe," "people," "nation," and "civil society." In his book *Ethnos and Society* (2018), Dugin traces the development of the varieties of human coexistence and integrates them into his thought.[1] In doing so, not only do his non-linear view of time and his critique of Western materialism and universalism become more intelligible, but his work also represents a sociologically founded criticism of the liberal-modern ideas of progress and individualism. Starting from the founder of ethnosociology, the Viennese Richard Thurnwald, Dugin explains that ethnosociology is not just another sub-discipline of sociology. Rather, it is about tracing the most important steps in the development of human societies. However, whereas modern sociology bases itself on the Western nation-state and nation, taking these as the norm, ethnosociology takes the smallest unit of human communities, ethnicity (ἔθνος *ethnos*), as the starting point.

Ethnicity is related to tribal society, the first level of human society. According to Dugin, this form of premodern community is an extremely conservative one. Its goal is the eternal return of the same,

---

1   Alexander Dugin, *Ethnos and Society* (London: Arktos, 2018).

the preservation of its original form. It is inherently, animistically grouped around a shaman, who forms the actual core of the tribal community, since he takes on the central role in its religious life; in the animistic sense, this is because nature itself is understood to be living and conscious. The ethnic kinship of this group, which numerically includes a few dozen people at most, is an indisputable reality. Rites accompany the passage into new stages of life. If a tribe member enters a new stage, a new identity is conferred to him, and thus he becomes a new man. If goods accumulate in this form of community, they are sacrificed in order to restore balance. Those led by shamanistic rituals and magic bring the world of ethnicity into balance time after time, whereby man and nature form a unit and merge into living space, the space in which man lives. With regard to the sense of time, there is no concept of history, nor of progress. Ethnicity does not know any idea of death, either. There is barely any form of hierarchy.

For Dugin, the closest analogue to this model is the theoretical idea of primeval communism as described by Karl Marx. The whole aim of a given ethnos is to prevent any serious modifications to itself. In the Potlatch ritual, for example, besides the ritual destruction of material abundance (or excess), one tries to keep the people's order as it is, in a process of "ethnostasis." This requires tremendous effort. If the ethnicity is faced by an outside threat, it is forced to establish a tight military organization. As part of this reorganization, the figure of the shaman is temporarily replaced by a warrior-king, who acts as the defender of the tribe. In this process, described by the liberal Ludwig Gumplowicz using the term "racial struggle" (*Rassenkampf*), the ethnos ultimately comes to dominate and subsume one or several tribes.

Through the ownership of slaves, primeval communism ceases to exist in terms of ethnicity, and a hierarchical society emerges. In the Indo-European case, this resulted from the emergence of the three-caste society, with priests at the head, followed by a warrior caste, and peasants who were taken from conquered tribes. Henceforth, we can speak of the next stage in the ethno-sociological development of a people. Whereas the animistic ideas of ethnicity lived on in the peasant caste, the community came to be dominated by a monotheistic faith. In economic life, the peasants diverted their surpluses to the cities, where the priests and warriors lived; in turn, the latter higher casts defended the peasants and ministered to their spiritual lives. This hierarchically structured community of people represents an organic whole, an alliance between elites and the masses. Religion, the economy, and everyday life are not separated from each other, but represent a unit that is given a context by religious faith and the hierarchy which it establishes. At its head sits a ruler who is seen as anointed by God. If ethnicity did not yet possess an awareness of history and death, these ideas surface in the people, with death and history having been grounded in the notion of a transcendental kingdom of heaven.

This is where empires emerge for the first time, federally structured and comprised of several peoples. One example of this form of rule is the Holy Roman Empire. While the peasants lived in the country, the priests and warriors resided in the cities. From a sociological point of view, the bourgeoisie emerged from conditions in which the warrior caste had to take peasant sons for the administration of the cities. The citizens were thus neither peasants nor warriors, but an alienated social class in between, able to attain a kind of power that went far beyond their social position, by means of early mercantile capitalism and the dominant position it afforded them as economic administrators. Subsequently, the bourgeoisie developed the will to rule itself. In the name of the modern ideas of liberalism and capitalism, it degraded the priesthood, annihilated the nobility, and waged war against the peasants, as can be seen in the example of the French Revolution. Instead of the three-caste system, the sole rule of the bourgeoisie came into being. It was this system which subsequently tried to impose its mercantilist values on all people in a given society, making, as it were, a bourgeois of everyone.

The bourgeoisie's ascendancy constituted a tremendous incursion into and usurpation of traditional society, and was therefore a cultural genocide against the premodern community of the people. But, in order to avoid drifting into total anarchy and a war of all against all, as already feared by Thomas Hobbes, the bourgeoisie was forced to forge an artificial group identity. The most artificial characteristic of this form of coexistence can be identified in the manner by which the modern nation opposes itself to ethnicity; what results is a people who can hardly be described as an ethnically homogenous group. The first modern society, which went beyond the scope of the people, was the nation, manifested politically in the form of the nation-state. As part of the social contract in this modern polity, all citizens were made to relinquish their power to the sovereign for the sake of societal stabilization. From the outset, the nation's only purpose was to provide the citizen with a structure for his constant enlightenment, the ultimate result of which was to be the totally liberated individual. The individual was the new man of liberal society, to be liberated from every form of collective identity (collective identity being the only real identity in the true sense of the word).

The interpretation of history also changes in the context of modern society. For the first time, linear historical thought appears in the context of modernity, which treats the end of history as its final destination. As part of the Enlightenment and its process of radical individuation, religion is first to be abolished, then the people, and finally national consciousness. After the nation, which defines itself through an artificially defined collective identity, comes civil society. Defined solely by the status of citizenship, the "civil society" has no other foundation than a legalistic social contract, unbeholden to any essential national identity. Its aim is to replicate itself around the world by abolishing all nation-states and borders. In the end, its purveyors seek to build a global society characterized by even greater centralization, as well as control over the planet's "citizens." As ethnic origins and culture no longer play a role in this model, replaced as these are by the economic power of the individual, the new elite now advocates mass migration from all parts of the world and the institution of a "global village." The Great Replacement is first carried out through mass immigration, then continues on to replacing these "diverse" populations with fleets of robots. The final aim of this process is the destruction of all remaining collective bonds existing in society. Egalitarianism knows no limits in this regard, and thus it also strives to abolish the family and gender identity on its way to the absolute individual. The object of this global state structure is no longer solely direct control over the life of the citizen, but violence against the citizen's soul by means of therapeutic psycho-politics. Whoever fails to submit to globalist dogma ends up socially marginalized. The needs of the citizen are steered towards consumption; the economy usurps politics. It is no longer the politicians but global corporations which decide the developmental direction of society.

Here, liberalism reaches its openly totalitarian phase, while making progressively less effort to maintain its façade of democracy. At this point, Dugin tells us, the West begins to transition from the model of nation-states to that of civil society; the European Union and the UN are to be seen as prototypes for a future global state. This transition marks the change from modernity into postmodernity. At this juncture, only one step remains towards the liberation of the individual: the human must cease to be human. Consequently, the postmodern society or simply the post-society, which remains the elites' vision of the future, is bereft of humans. In the thinking of postmodern and post-humanist thinkers such as Raymond Kurzweil and Reza Negarestani, the human will be replaced by cyborgs, chimeras, and artificial intelligence. The outcome of the modern age is not a prosperous future, but rather the end of the individual. If the development from premodernity to modernity was marked by an explosion of ethnicity, which sought to expand the characteristics of the tribal society on increasingly greater scales, then the path from modernity to postmodernity is marked by an implosion of the individual and of ethnicity. The individual is actually not "indivisible," as its name implies, but is further split into the dividual. Then, as per Deleuze and Guattari, hands and feet rebel against the dictatorship of the brain; schizophrenia is celebrated as further liberation and emancipation.

Is this development into madness inevitable? Alexander Dugin answers this question emphatically in the negative in his final lecture on ethnosociology[2]. The existence of ethnicities in Oceania and the Amazon rainforest proves to us that this development is not our inevitable fate. In the same way, peoples and traditional societies still in existence today can be found in the Arabian Gulf as well as in the "archeomodern" states of Russia and India, where modernity is present only as a thin veneer. Even the nation-state can be sustained, provided a political will is formed that wants to defend it. A return to premodernity, to the people and their community, is also possible. The resurgence of civilizations, the populist moment in Europe, and the renaissance of traditional religions are all signs of the rebirth of the premodern in the face of the West's slipping into postmodernity. But the fight against postmodernity is not a walk in the park, just as a global retrogression to premodernity is not inevitable. Rather, it requires that one consciously take up the spiritual battle against postmodernity in all its manifestations for the sake of the world's re-enchantment.

---

2   Alexander Dugin, "Ethnosociology. Final conclusions" (2013) [https://www.youtube.com/watch?v=r2P6XokZ7gk].

Noomakhia: The War of Ideas

W HILE Alexander Dugin's geopolitical theses and his *Fourth Political Theory* enjoy a certain degree of familiarity in Europe and the West, his *magnum opus* on the "war of ideas," *Noomakhia* [*Ноомахия*], remains largely unknown. This work, which now comprises more than 30 volumes, builds on Noology, a term derived from the ancient Greek terms *nous* (νοῦς), meaning mind, attention, awareness, and *logos* (λόγος), meaning word, speech, discourse. Of course, the present scope does not allow us to go into the details of this monumental opus of Dugin's, but we will nonetheless seek to provide a rough summary of it, based on his introductory lectures[1] which outline the project.

The basis of Dugin's multipolar philosophy is his idea that there is no single, universal form of thought, but rather many different ways of thinking. Building on his ethnosociological work, Dugin assumes that the thinking of every people is unique. It is always just a different expression of the *nous*, but these characteristics have consequences for people's lives, thoughts, and sentiments. Furthermore, according to the Russian thinker, we are led to assume that every people also creates its own world through its unique thinking, something which Dugin calls the "existential horizon."

In *Noomakhia*, Dugin analyzes various specific cultures, dedicating himself to the study of not only the American, German, and

---

1   Alexander Dugin, "Noomachia (Serbia 2018) Lecture 1. Introduction," *Paideuma.tv* [https://paideuma.tv/en/video/noomachia-serbia-2018-lecture-1-introduction].

English cultures, but also to those many cultures within Russia, China, and Africa. In his multilevel analysis, he incorporates elements from philosophy, ethnology, and anthropology, as well as geopolitics, sociology, Ferdinand de Saussure's structuralism, the phenomenological thought of Husserl and Heidegger, as well as the mythological studies of Georges Dumézil. According to Dugin, who engages Nietzsche's division of cultures into Apollonian and Dionysian, the *Nous* manifests itself in three main forms with many subdivisions: the Logos of Apollo, the Logos of Dionysus, and the Logos of Cybele. The *Nous* would be unable to manifest itself without one of these three *logoi*. In every culture, all three are represented, and no culture can exist with only two *logoi*. Ultimately, it is the manner in which the *logoi* are combined in every culture which prevents any one of them from taking precedence. However, Dugin does not assume a peaceful coexistence between them; rather, they are locked in a constant struggle for dominance. It is this incessant agonism which inspired Dugin's title for the series.

This fight is not about final but temporary victories. The Logos of Apollo embodies light, the transcendence, the heavenly father, and patriarchy. Dionysus, on the other hand, does not represent darkness, but rather shadow, the masculine in a feminine reality, immanent transcendence. The complete absence and the dark night, on the other hand, would be embodied by the Logos of the Cybele, an ancient Anatolian mother goddess who existed well before the Hittites. It is within Cybele that radical immanence manifests itself, along with the titanic element and matriarchal feminism.

The Logos of the Indo-Europeans has been decisive in the noological formation of Europe. The origin of this logos lies with the "Turanian" peoples, whose primordial homeland (*Urheimat*) lay south of the Urals; this Logos is, moreover, based on the Kurgan hypothesis of Marija Gimbutas, according to whom the Turanians were not a Turkic people, but were instead Indo-European nomads. These cattle herders colonized large parts of Eurasia, beginning with the

Turanian lands, by means of the horse, which they were the first to domesticate. In the East, their expansion reached all the way to India, while in the West their terminus was the British Isles. They underwent three stages of culture, according to Leo Frobenius: first, they developed a fascination for the sun; then, they began to express this obsession artistically; finally, they implemented it technologically in the form of the wheel which, as part of the chariot, allowed the Indo-Europeans to expand in all directions like the rays of the sun. This expansion was also spiritual in nature, as the French mythographer Georges Dumézil makes clear in his study of Indo-European ideology.

According to Dumézil, this ruling ideology was articulated in three castes: the first caste was comprised of the monarchy and priesthood, who were seen as sacred and above the merely human level. They were served by the second caste, the warrior caste, which ensured the loyalty of the third caste of cattle herders to the first. The entire society formed an army that pursued wisdom and bravery as supreme values. Here, we see a unified society shaped entirely by the Apollonian Logos. Their cities were enclosed by walls and served as fortresses. According to Dumézil, all Indo-European societies are erected vertically, which finds its expression in language, culture, as well as our view of history. The gender relations therein are clearly patriarchal, but the friendship between man and woman is informed by what Dugin calls "anagylany,"[2] which integrated women as strong and full-fledged members of society amidst the background of male dominance. In Plato's thinking, Alexander Dugin recognizes the pure Logos of Apollo. Plato's cosmology assumes that everything from heaven returns to heaven. Its temporal reference for the past,

---

2   Dugin employs this neologism in contrast to Maria Gimbutas' notion of "gylany," which denotes the dominance of woman over man, framed by friendly relations between the two sexes under a matriarchy. Dugin's term denotes a patriarchal society characterized by friendly rapport between the sexes, whereby the feminine is not totally in submission to the masculine.

the present, and the future is fixed to eternity. According to Dugin, Christianity's elements of logoi-proportions are also embodied in pure Platonism. Thus, Christianity does not represent a break with Indo-European history, but rather its continuation.

How, then, did the Europe of today come about? It is the result of the Indo-Europeans' conquest of paleo-Europe. In stark contrast to its conquerors, the original peoples of the continent were matriarchal in character. At the center of this civilization stood the Anatolian mother-goddess, Cybele. The Logos of Cybele instituted a different view of the world: in agrarian-sedentary society, cities without walls acted as centers, women dominated agriculture, in which no animals were employed, and it was believed that everything originated out of a primeval substance. At its center stood the Mother-Goddess who gave birth to and devoured everything. Under the Cybelean Logos, the cosmos has its center in the interior of the earth, instead of in heaven. Consequently, the kingdom of the mother was opposed to that of the father. It did not know any immortal soul; rather, the same substance remains in a perpetual state of being born and dying. In the myth of Attis, we find the origin of a self-castrating priestly caste which venerates the matriarchy of the mother-goddess Cybele, performing orgies and blood sacrifices. The center of this civilization in Europe is believed to have been what is now the Serbian site of Lepenski Vir, the oldest city in Europe.

If we keep this coming-into-being of Europe in mind, we discover that European society has two levels: the vertical, patriarchal level of the Indo-Europeans and the subjugated Paleo-European, matriarchal civilization. Thus, every Indo-European culture is seen as the result of a mixture or superposition of these two *logoi*, which occurred as the Indo-European nomads settled down and took over agriculture. This coming together of the Logos of Apollo and the Logos of Cybele took place about 3,000 years ago. On the battlefield of the two *logoi*, the Logos of Dionysus finally emerged. In this Dionysian Logos, the spiritual conquest of Paleo-Europe by the Indo-Europeans reaches its greatest clarity. At the same time, the Dionysian Logos is an opening for the act of interpretation, which gains sovereignty in itself. In the Indo-European context, Dionysus is always a god who appears together with Apollo. It is only here that we encounter the Dionysian Logos in its pure form; unlike in China, this form is never dominant in the purely Indo-European context. At this stage of mixture, the cults of Cybele were reinterpreted in the light of Apollo, and the unbridled Cybele became the tamed Demeter. But this fight for interpretation can never conclude. Just as Dionysus can be imagined as a god who descends from heaven to earth to conquer the underworld, he can also be imagined as rising from the underworld to Olympus and fighting the gods. According to Dugin, the possibility of a dark double remains open, that of Adonis instead of Dionysus. The Logos of Cybele, therefore, has never disappeared from European thought, but rather has been preserved in the peasantry which, in its role as the third estate, sustained the Cybelean impulse at the margins of society. As Dugin claims, European civilization is concerned at its core with the problem of Dionysus, which has found different expressions among the various European peoples.

In contrast to historians and thinkers of the liberal Right, Dugin does not refer to a "Judeo-Christian Occident" as the root of European civilization, but shows that the decisive influence in the formation of traditional Medieval society in Europe was Hellenism. The intellectual current emerging from Alexander the Great's conquest of the Achaemenid Persian Empire, ruling at that time over Asia Minor, Egypt, the Arabian Peninsula, and Persia, as well as present-day Pakistan, is held by Dugin to be the decisive impetus in the creation of European civilization. At the same time, Hellenism took over the Iranized space and Iranian thought (Dugin considers Iranism *vis-à-vis* Iranians to stand in the same relationship as Hellenism does to the Greeks), borrowing from its concepts of history—completely unknown to Europeans until then—the figure of the Messiah and a dualistic worldview. With that came a concept of evil, understood not as a simple obstacle (as was the case in the thought of the Turanians or the Brahmins), but as a mortal opponent. Hellenistic thought spread across Europe on the backs of the Roman Legions, where it laid the foundation for the European Logos. In the Greek mysteries of Dionysus and Demeter, one can recognize a prefiguration of the Christian mysteries of the body and blood of God. The Romans added the important figure of the Imperator, who played the Christian role of the *katekhon*, the "restrainer" of the Antichrist and guardian of peace within the Empire.

Whereas there was a continuity of the imperial idea in the Eastern Roman Empire until the final Roman collapse (the fall of Constantinople in 1453), this idea vanished in Western Europe already in 476, until it was restored with a *translatio imperii* constituted by the coronation of Charlemagne in 800. It is no accident that Christianity was born in the Hellenistic-Mediterranean space; rather, this should be seen as a natural consequence of the Indo-European Logos. From a noological point of view, we also discover here the Apollonian Logos, with a heavenly Holy Father and Creator God, whose Son is the embodiment of transcendental immanence and, in the Apollonian sense, a purified form of Dionysus, as well as the woman in Apollonian interpretation, who takes the form of the Virgin Mary. The trifunctional division into priests, warriors, and peasants was also preserved in Christian society. While Christianity remained stable within the framework of Orthodoxy in the East, it metamorphosed strongly in a dualistic direction during the Great Schism of 1054, when the West and East severed their communion.

Protestantism, on the other hand, can be viewed in two conflicting ways: on the one hand, Proto-Protestantism, with its criticism of the corrupt Catholic Church and its emphasis on introspection, can be compared with the "third man" idea expressed by mystics such as Meister Eckhardt; this "third man" embodies the radical self, which stands in direct relationship to God and is different from the "first man" (the animal aspect of man) and the "second man" (the rational aspect of man); this point, lying hidden in the soul, was nonetheless abandoned by Protestants in favor of the "second man." For Protestants, the aim was to achieve a direct connection to God, something which Dugin views as the product of titanic arrogance. This led to a transformation of the *logos* in early Protestantism, radicalized in Calvinism, which in turn proclaimed the "second man" to be the only human dimension and consequently denied the presence of the sacred in the world. Thus, Protestantism represents the crack in the great structure of the Western Christian tradition, which led to its destruction further down the line, and created the preconditions for the beginning of modernity.

In modernity, Alexander Dugin sees the revenge of the Cybelean Logos. The Logos of Cybele is not the only one available to us, but is rather the basis of a specific society, structure, and horizon of existence which is radically different from the traditional society of the European Middle Ages. Cybele's current reign dawned at the end of the Middle Ages and reached its full onset with the Renaissance. Building on the criticism of postmodernists directed towards modernity, Dugin points out that modern society did not replace traditional society by virtue of representing higher truth, but rather by virtue of fielding better propagandists. Modernity benefited from the fact that the worldview of European peoples had completely changed by the time of the Renaissance. At the center of modernity stood the bourgeoisie, the people of the city. Here, we are speaking of the *idiotes* (or the "private individual") in the Hellenic sense, an individual detached from all ties, belonging neither to the peasant caste (from which he usually came), nor to the warrior caste which he had previously served. As a servant of the warrior caste, he was employed in the administration of the cities, which were organized as fortresses and administrative centers. There, he acted as a merchant, viewed with abhorrence by those who still identifiably belonged to one of the three estates.

Over the course of modernity, the bourgeoisie came to seize power in two different ways: either in an evolutionary way (as in England) or in a revolutionary way (as in France). Whereas the English path was strongly shaped by Protestant religion, and a gradual replacement of the old order took place, the revolutionary fury of the bourgeoisie in France was violently unleashed from the very outset against the priesthood, nobility, and peasantry. The spiritual revolution which preceded the political one was nurtured by the anti-Christian philosophy of modernity; it was this new philosophy which destroyed the Christian worldview and displaced its attendant Apollonian and Dionysian Logoi. Among the culprits of this transformation was the critique of Aristotle and Scholasticism which destroyed the theocentric worldview. God was no longer acknowledged to be the unmoved mover at the center of creation, and Divine reason was replaced by simple human reason. The Earth was no longer a perfect manifestation of God's will, but had been reduced to an accidental orb, revolving around an indifferent sun, according to the newly advanced scientific theories of Galileo and Copernicus.

In Dugin's *Noomakhia*, we can see that modernity is not just nihilistic, but that it follows its own Cybelean logic. According to Dugin, we are not encountering something new in modernity, but are merely remembering the old Logos of Cybele. The types of the Cybelean Logos include the evolutionist worldview, the atomistic school of Democritus, Epicurus, and Lucretius, and the return of the latter in the works of Thomas Hobbes, René Descartes, Robert Boyle, Sir Isaac Newton, and Pierre Gassendi. Thus, the atomists assumed that species were mixed at the beginning and only gradually evolved into the creatures we know today. It was their conviction that the gods, too, were mortal. This materialistic "myth" of the purely Cybelean worldview was rediscovered in the Renaissance, and gradually sanitized of its mythical elements. The transcendent and anti-materialistic worldview of Christianity was thus stealthily replaced by the radically immanent and materialistic worldview of modernity.

In the process of this transformation and replacement, the state was also de-Christianized. In place of the *Imperium*, with the Emperor acting in the religious role of *katekhon*, came the secular state. This state was erected from the bottom up through a social contract among individuals, meant to protect them from Hobbes's "war of all against all." It was Hobbes who likened the modern state to a mechanical snake or dragon, the so-called "Leviathan." Since it was built by individuals and only served to liberate trade and economic activity for the citizenry, this new model of the state lacked any notion of transcendence. In contrast to the Imperium, the modern state is secular and tolerates all religions while expelling the priesthood from government. The warrior nobility is replaced by soldiers, whose weapons the state can take away as soon as their services should prove unnecessary. This distinguishes the soldier from the warrior, whose weapons remain permanently in his possession. The political ideology of liberalism that emerged from the Enlightenment, in which the thought of modernity was systematized, was from the very beginning a glorification of the *idiotes* in the form of the bourgeoisie. This novel subject was idiosyncratically glorified by all three of the modern ideologies: whereas, in liberalism, the peasants were drawn to the city, where they became wealthy, private citizens, communism forced them into cities, making them into a poor bourgeoisie called the "proletariat," which was ultimately agitated into overthrowing the rich bourgeoisie; and in nationalism, which later gave rise to fascism and National Socialism, the citizen was encouraged to be chauvinistic, for the sake of an artificial, national collective. Here, too, the peasants were treated as second-class citizens, perceived simply as elements living between the cities.

The modern age persists on the basis of an anti-Christian scientific worldview, the modern state, the destruction of the three Indo-European castes, and a constantly alleged improvement of humanity within the framework of progress. What is it, then, which has allowed postmodernity to succeed modernity? In Dugin's eyes, postmodernity concerns itself with purging the last remnants of traditional societies that have survived into the modern age. While modernity focused on establishing the rule of reason, postmodernism rebelled against this dictatorship of reason. The central thinkers in this new chapter of *Noomakhia* are, according to Dugin, Gilles Deleuze and Félix Guattari, who founded the so-called "schizophrenic revolution." In their appeal to contemporary "discoveries" in neurology, they argue that human rationality only accounts for the male pole of reason. In their demand for a female psychoanalysis, they discovered two psychological systems: the "paranoid" and the "schizophrenic." While the paranoid system is hierarchically structured, the schizophrenic system is more feminist and egalitarian, based on an inner division of self. This propagation of the schizophrenic system in turn led the two thinkers to fight against the dictatorship of the brain. The individual (who, as the name states, cannot be divided) is to be replaced by the "dividual" (the individual divided by postmodern paradigms); likewise, the dictatorship of the brain is to be replaced by a "parliament of organs." Finally, the most radical concepts of postmodernism also view the concept of the "organism" as fascistic, and therefore advocate for a "body without organs" (BWO), formless and centerless. Instead of the corporeal, "arboreal" model, what Deleuze and Guattari propose is a purely horizontal scheme of perpetual dislocation and migration. They call this network the "rhizome," which is taken to be the definitive replacement for the individual. This network, named after a Greek word which describes a subterranean mass of roots, is meant topologically to depict the new (non-)structure of postmodern society.

This new materialism is not about things in themselves, but about something that is lower than all things. From a Traditionalist point of view, Dugin claims, what Deleuze and Guattari describe is the intracorporeal plane inhabited by the beings of the underworld. The rhizome does not communicate between individuals, but between their organs in a completely schizophrenic way. Further, Deleuze and Guattari call for the liberation of the mind from the body, so that desires can enter the "parliament of organs." In all of these reflections, the differences between classical liberalism and post-liberalism are especially pronounced. As Paul Edward Gottfried has written in *Multiculturalism and the Politics of Guilt: Towards a Secular Theocracy*, post-liberalism is the result of a hybridization of liberalism and cultural Marxism.[3] Several paradigm shifts have occurred in the wake of this development: while the old liberalism was concerned with the individual, post-liberalism concerns itself with the dividual; artificial intelligence replaces the intellect; the network replaces normal relationships; and virtuality replaces reality. While online profiles today make it possible for us to adopt a different personality, the 3D printer could soon allow us to fabricate custom, artificial bodies.

According to Dugin, what this process entails is an emulation of the corporeal principle: we lose the individual and become, instead, an agglomeration of disjunct objects. The only barrier to this transformation at present is the relatively rudimentary state of AI. While a weak AI has already been developed for administrative functions, one expects to see the eventual development of an Artificial General Intelligence (AGI), which not only possesses the properties of human intelligence, but vastly surpasses them; according to Raymond Kurzweil, the inflection point of AGI's emergence is the "singularity," which he has predicted will occur in the year 2045. At the moment of singularity, progress will reach a hitherto unprecedented scale, and AI will become self-replicating. This event will be marked by the appearance of a posthuman species. If in the modern age one viewed evolution from animals to humans as a result of progress, then the next leap in this trajectory is seen by posthumanists as the singularity itself. This development and its advancement have become the goal of the present philosophical current known as accelerationism. The result of this cataclysm will be a total redefinition of the human

---

3   Paul Edward Gottfriend, *Multiculturalism and the Politics of Guilt: Towards a Secular Theocracy* (University of Missouri Press, 2002).

being—and such a new definition will have to account for new possibilities, such as that of artificially reproducing the human brain. But, in order for this to be achieved, man himself must first become a machine. One step in this direction is political correctness, which conditions those under its sway to think "correctly." In the new totalitarianism, every person who speaks out against progress and political correctness will be (or already is) devalued as "non-human." According to Dugin, this reflects liberalism's totalitarian aspirations: one is allowed to be liberal, left-liberal and right-liberal, but anything outside of this framework is proscribed.

This regulation of thinking requires increasingly more absurd forms of propaganda. For example, despite the continued lack of evidence that Russia significantly interfered in the 2016 US presidential election, mainstream media outlets such as *The New York Times* and *The Washington Post* unabashedly continue to evoke the conspiracy theory as though it were inarguably true. As Dugin sees it, what lies behind such discourses is an algorithm which attempts to emulate an impression of the status quo—"reality" is besides the point. Here, virtuality supersedes reality. However, even more devastating and challenging is the fact that the concept of "reality" as such is a product of early modernity, rendering any attempt to defend it illogical. In the traditional, Apollonian worldview, metaphysical Ideas were the founts of being and life, while their reflections as earthly objects were relegated to a lesser status. In the traditional sense, reality drew its facticity from its having been created by God. In the modern age, however, reality was accepted as such—Man as such, and the world as such, without an author, without a creator. Reason draws a demarcation line between people and the metaphysical reasons for their existence. In this manner, reality is already virtuality. With the advent of postmodernity, this transition from reality to virtuality was only made explicit. Metaphysically speaking, we cannot save reality until we save spirituality.

In traditional European metaphysics, "reality" was not taken as a basis in and of itself, but rather was based on pre-real, pre-temporal Ideas. If the Ideas fall away, we are left only with that which is virtual, emulated. Thus, postmodernity represents the logical conclusion of modernity. According to Dugin, postmodernism itself is characterized by an absolute dominance of the Cybelean Logos. Postmodern feminism is not about equality, but the total destruction of men and masculinity. While, at the beginning of modernity, man saw material limits set upon him in the sense of the matriarchal type of citizen, and saw the discrediting of the archetypes of priest, monk, and warrior, the postmodern era saw not only his emasculation, but also the discrediting of female happiness derived from motherhood. Instead, woman was given the will to power, a blind pursuit of power for power's sake. Dugin, following René Guénon, recognizes a principle of feminine power which, should it turn away from its masculine counterpart, must inevitably degenerate into a blind, demiurgic monstrosity. The recognition of homosexuality as normal must ultimately lead to a catastrophic imbalance between the sexes. The victory of Cybele in the sexual field does not consist in a victory of the feminine, but in the collapse of sexuality itself. Hence, the transition from modernity to postmodernity constitutes a supersession of the atomistic, individualistic society by the "-tomistic," "-dividual" society.[4]

This pure cosmopolitanism knows no borders, races, or *ethnoi*, nor does it value individual freedom anymore, instead replacing it with the free flow of networks. The outcome is an AI matrix which, so the thinking goes, will have replaced the mortal human body with an immortal machine. The last frontier of individual liberation

---

4   A rich interpretation of Apollonian femininity and the "war of the sexes" from the perspective of neo-Eurasianism and the New Right is presented in the works of Alexander Dugin's daughter, Daria Platonova Dugina, who was deeply engaged with the French *Nouvelle Droite*. See: Daria Platonova Dugina, *Eschatological Optimism* (PRAV Publishing, 2023), especially "Part II: The Feminine Principle and the Problem of the Subject"; idem, *A Theory of Europe: A View of the New Right* (Arktos, 2024).

is liberation from the collective human identity altogether. This also implies an end of *logos*. Given the imminent date of the singularity, little time remains for a return to Tradition and a revolt against (post) modernity.

As Dugin tells us, conservative societies like Russia are not good role models here, as they only succeed in impeding the crawl toward singularity without suspending it. For Dugin, Russia may say no to postmodernism, but it has yet to formulate an alternative to it. The Russian state is anti-accelerationist in nature, not for the sake of rejecting further progress towards postmodernity and advocating for a defense of reality (which it also, paradoxically, rejects), but in order to persist in its status as an archeomodern society. From this emerges its "archeomodern" character, since its elite is modernistic and materialistic but does not wish to suffer the ultimate consequences of this development in the form of postmodernism. Only the country's traditional Orthodox clergy advocates on the margins of society for a return to traditional society. Dugin insists that although Russia is only apparently conservative-revolutionary, it holds great potential for something more. The Russian people continue to bear their *katekhonic* mission, based on the Dionysian Logos — even if this Logos has fallen into deep slumber, it has not yet been entirely lost.

The West has decided to finalize postmodernity; this decision lends extreme gravity to Heidegger's insistence that "only a God can save us." Russia, on the other hand, still has the possibility to say "no." One possibility of spiritual resistance which Dugin has identified is the task of carrying on Heidegger's project of an "other beginning" of philosophy, which entails further elaborating the Dionysian Logos, philosophically grasping Chaos, and discovering the "Radical Self." The figure of this project and revolt is that of Dionysus travailing through the Cybelean night of postmodernism.

Actors of the German New Right: Götz Kubitschek and the Institute for State Policy

THE PUBLISHER Götz Kubitschek is one of the best-known representatives of the New Right in Germany. Born in Ravensburg in 1970, Kubitschek was deployed abroad in Bosnia from 1997 to 1998 as part of his commission in the German armed forces (the *Bundeswehr*). He increased his journalistic commitments as editor of the weekly newspaper Young Freedom (*Junge Freiheit*), where he has been active since 1993. In his role as editor, he not only popularized thinkers of the Conservative Revolution like Ernst Jünger and Ernst von Salomon, but also acted as temporary lead-editor of the journal's security and military section. Together with Karl-Heinz Weissman, who also came from the entourage of Young Freedom, in 2000 Kubitschek founded the Institute for State Policy (*Institut für Staatspolitik* — IfS), an organization that clearly situates itself within the New Right. His main field of activity continues to be editorial in nature, as he directs the activities of the journal *Sezession* and the publishing house Antaios. While Götz Kubitschek ranks as one of the best-known representatives of a New Right in Germany today, it is interesting that he is unaffiliated with the French *Nouvelle Droite*. Instead, he orients himself towards the tradition of Conservative Revolution.

In addition to his publishing and journalistic activities, Kubitschek also frequently engages in activism. In addition to his well-known appearances as a speaker for PEGIDA, he is also a founding member of the organization Conservative-Subversive Action

(*Konserative-Subversive Aktion,* KSA). This activist group, centered around the activities of Kubitschek and Felix Menzel, takes its name from the New-Left "Subversive Action" of the 1960s. The KSA carried out more than a dozen actions from 2006 to 2010, disrupting events held by the the radical Left, such as the "1968 Congress" of an organization affiliated with the Left party (*Die Linke*) and readings by Günther Grass. The KSA has also protested against German foreign policy and its politics of memory, such as when Angela Merkel paid state visit to Paris on the occasion of ceremonies commemorating the end of the First World War.

Kubitschek's volume *Provokation*, which appeared as part of the *Kaplaken* book series, is a guide to resistance. As the name of the volume suggests, one ought not to participate in the discourse, but rather disrupt it. Divided into the chapters "We—Resolution," "You—Hesitation," "I—Begin," "You—Jump," Kubitschek's book carries out a ruthless analysis of the situation in Germany and of his own political camp, calling for a disruption of social consensus. In the first section of *Provokation*, Kubitschek laments the cozy death of the Germans. Instead of acting upon outrage, they have simply been deprived of their fate, sedated with warm housing, gaming consoles, and a plentiful supply of food and drink. But, as if the passivity of the masses did not cause enough harm already, the political wing of the German Right also remains weak and fragmented (Kubitschek is writing well before the political successes of the AfD). The time to prepare for Germany's future is rapidly running out, and no one has taken any action.[1]

So, what is to be done? Given the situation, one should have no fear of any radical change in Germany. The only time to despair is when one discovers that the youth of our nation no longer possess the strength for an upheaval. Germany is terminally ill and, in view of this condition, it would greatly benefit from a crisis, as resignation

---

1   Götz Kubitschek, *Provokation* (Schnellroda: Antaios, 2007), 7.

to an imminent end is still preferable to maintaining a drip-feed of entropy. Drawing on the works of Jakob Burckhardt, a forerunner of the Conservative Revolution, Kubitschek describes the crisis as a feverish state and a crossroads at which the sick body of the nation must be tried in order to see whether it still has enough strength to recover. In doing so, it is important for one to resolve either to lead a mature life which has overcome crisis, or to plunge back into crisis.[2] This implies not worrying about some abstract future prosperity (and, here, the author means the prosperous future of multicultural consumer society), but about a specifically German future, which requires that the German people continue to live on German soil.[3] Faced with mass immigration, Germany finds itself in the opening stages of a civil war.[4] This conflict is characterized by latent lines of conflict within the multicultural society, which can either be affirmed or denied. But despair is not an option. All one can do is face the crisis and seek the recovery of the nation, so that it can rediscover itself and resume its mantle as the center of Europe. It is imperative to plant incendiary ideas and muster new courage, as well as to mobilize against tolerance and creeping decay, argues Kubitschek.[5] The current multicultural system does not offer any acceptable future. Either it continues as a multicultural society designed for employment and consumption, or one of the more demographically dynamic ethnic groups must seize the opportunity with both hands and organize the state differently. For Germans, this would mean internal displacement, crime, violence, civilizational regress, and worse.[6] Faced with this, Germans can either resist or face extinction. While Jean Raspail's novel *The Camp of the Saints* provides a cautionary tale for how Europeans might disappear, resistance can only ever be action,

---

2   Ibid., 8.

3   Ibid., 9.

4   Ibid., 10.

5   Ibid., 13.

6   Ibid., 16.

not discussion. Above all, Kubitschek argues, what Europe needs is a spiritual civil war, to be waged against the lobbyists of decomposition. It is Germans themselves, and no one else, who have enabled this destructive social experiment.

In opposition to this stands the eponymous chapter "We — Resolution." "We" includes those Germans who recognize the situation and can present complex issues in a simplified manner. Herein, Kubitschek clearly refers to the thinking of the New Right when he seeks for the reasons for Germany's decline in the Germans themselves, while simultaneously attempting to pinpoint the main enemy, whom he does not identify as the immigrants, but as ethnically German collaborators. Kubitschek derives two fundamental tasks from this position: a sharpening of terms and an identification of the opponent.[7] It is important not to overestimate the effect of the written word and to keep in mind that what matters is action.[8] As the Right is forced into a weak position, provocation is the only effective method of garnering public attention. After having studied the reflexes of the media age, Kubitschek concludes that forcing public attention through a coup is the only way forward.[9] For the provocateur, it is important to appear in the media, because anything outside of the media space is excluded from the virtual world. Therefore, every provocation must be aimed at soliciting a reaction from the opponent. In order to be noticed, one must do the unexpected and deliberately violate the rules, particularly those which safeguard the current power structure.

In this manner, Kubitschek addresses the model of "rule by discourse," understood by Thor von Waldstein as the endless deferral of change by means of argument that is so essential to liberalism.[10]

---

7   Ibid., 20.

8   Ibid., 21.

9   Ibid., 23ff.

10   Ibid., 24.

One should not take the democratic consensus seriously, because it is fundamentally unserious in and of itself. For the democratic approach, provocations by artists and professed unconventional thinkers are required to break into the debate without disturbing the illusion of consensus. By contrast, Kubitschek understands provocation to be something fundamentally different from marketing strategy, which depends on acceptance into the public discourse. From the viewpoints of the soldier and the publisher, provocation constitutes the foreclosure of discourse as a form of consensus; in other words, provocation does not by one "standing room in the salon," but leads to a "termination of the party."[11] It requires that one follow Gottfried Benn's call to genuinely reject any desire for reconciliation with those who have caused Germany's current state and barge in as uninvited guest with uncomfortable questions wherever there is a strong consensus, confronting the "belle of the ball" about the bodies hidden in her basement.[12]

In the second chapter, "You — The Hesitation," Kubitschek addresses those who reject the provocation and proceeds to expound his philosophy of life. By employing the description of a young man suffering from the feverish wish to reconstitute Germany on the basis of a national imperative and bring on the end of history by means of a necessary Will to Power, we experience in just a few pages the failure of a young idealist at the hands of the grim realities on the ground. After two years, he once again finds himself in the position of the humiliated idealist, who has been offered exactly four options: a slide into cynicism, degradation into a senile laughingstock, a radicalization of his methods to the point of self-immolation or, finally, what Armin Mohler described as a "second birth," through which he finally realizes the essence of the Right. This argument is predicated on the insight that no single person can ever grasp, understand, or

---

11   Ibid., 25.

12   Ibid., 26.

control reality in its entirety.[13] This means the rejection of utopia as marshalling yard into the future, a farewell to political naiveté, and return to real life, in order to understand what is faulty and to make it viable.[14]

According to Mohler, history should be understood as a school of humility, against which all monocausal explanations are shattered, rendering the complex character of reality known to us. For the conservative, this way is difficult to define and not rationally explainable; it is a drive for affirmation.[15] It leads to the stock character of the gardener as sketched by Ernst Jünger, who realizes that the activist often acted in vain, proceeded too tumultuously and, in his naiveté, did things that he would have been better off not doing. The gardener is characterized by his dedication to form and design. Furthermore, he must understand that, in everyday life, all things of gravity — such as his understanding of the state — must take priority over his own life-style. Here, Kubitschek assumes a tightrope walk between necessary openness and tactical masking.[16] The provocation itself must always be commensurate, so that the provocateur does not lose his sense of proportion. Only by the personal example of a well-led life can one observe everything around and determine what is fruitful and corrosive. For this, it is necessary to open oneself up to the cosmos of right-wing thinking, which Kubitschek outlines with a list of thinkers belonging to the Conservative Revolution as well as other right-wing readings worthy of recommendation.[17]

---

13   Ibid., 35.

14   Ibid., 38.

15   Ibid., 39–40.

16   Ibid., 48–49.

17   Kubitschek refers to: Alfred Bäumler, Alain de Benoist, Gottfried Benn, Jacob Burckhardt, Emile Cioran, Helmut Diwald, Arnold Gehlen, Herbert Gruhl, Ernst and Friedrich Georg Jünger, Martin Heidegger, Kurt Hübner, Günther Maschke, Armin Mohler, Ernst von Salomon, Carl Schmitt, Robert Spaemann, Oswald Spengler, Karlheinz Weißmann, and Bernard Willms. Kubitschek

The third chapter, "I — Begin", consists initially of Kubitschek's autobiographical descriptions of his "second birth," which occurred during his readings Armin Mohler. Directing the reader's attention to Mohler's popularization of the term "Conservative Revolution," the author demonstrates the necessity of weaponizing language to the tactical advantage of one's own side. Instrumental in such a weaponization is the creation of new terms and their dissemination, as well as the laying of a solid foundation from which to define one's own position.[18] To this he adds his concept of the "recklessness of the rapid advance,"[19] understood as a resolute, unconventional attack meant to stall the enemy, and the "liberation of the *Gestalt*,"[20] meaning the removal of an essential point from a complex context. In reply to the decadent loss of reality, Kubitschek proposes the esteem of form, expressed as a tragic position ("and yet they held up their swords"[21]) and a stylistic awareness. All of this leads to a tactics of nonconformity, manifested as a genuine appreciation for plurality.[22]

At the end of *Provokation*, Kubitschek explains that he does not wish to subordinate the tactic of provocation to a strategy, as this would rob the provocation of its independence. He advocates for physical fitness, general self-improvement, and emotional continence. The accomplishment of these three goals results in a merging of politics, art, and an awareness of one's own "I." In its provocative

---

further argues that novels are even better suited than theoretical writings for the search for the right balance, citing *Der Vater* (The Father) by Jochen Klepper, *Die Kinder Finsternis* (The Children of Darkness) by Wolf von Niebelschütz, *Der Großtyrann und das Gericht* (The Great Tyrant and the Court) by Werner Bergengruen, *Die vierzig Tage des Musa Dagh* (The Forty Days of Musa Dagh) by Franz Werfel, *Jürg Jenatsch* by Gottfried Keller, and *Die schwarze Weide* (The Black Willow) by Horst Lange.

18   Kubitschek, *Provokation*, 57.

19   Ibid., 54.

20   Ibid., 56.

21   "*Dennoch die Schwerter halten*" — the title of a poem by Gottfried Benn.

22   Kubitschek, *Provokation*, 60.

form, the political becomes art and the illustration of the will to form, the formative, stylistic awareness of an "I" which aspires to self-expression.[23] But this "I" should not dwell on the level of the individual ego, as in an expression of "I do not"; rather, it should multiply itself on the level of the people into the expression of "neither do we."[24]

The chapter "You — Jump" marks the end of the "provocation." It leads the reader to a final, decisive question: Are "you" ready to burst into some place uninvited and hurl your "not-I" at people?[25] The provocation is aimed not only outwardly for the sake of escalation, confrontation, and the attraction of attention, but also inwardly, in order to set an example, mobilize, and recruit. Here, it suffices to tear a political milieu out of its lethargy and overcome its defeatism. The "leap" that everyone must undertake consists in becoming a signpost oneself, an island of resistance that can indicate the way for others, prefiguring a different possibility.[26]

---

23 Ibid., 63.

24 Ibid., 69.

25 Ibid., 71.

26 Ibid., 76–77.

Philip Stein, Jungeuropa, and
the One Percent Network

THE YOUNG publisher and activist Philip Stein (1991-) stands out among the German representatives of the New Right who, on the one hand, orient themselves towards the French *Nouvelle Droite* and, on the other hand, have lost sight neither of the social dimension of this milieu, nor of its European context. Stein first published his work in Felix Menzel's *Blaue Narzisse* (*Blue Daffodil*) magazine, with whom he also co-authored the volume *Young Europe: Scenarios of Upheaval* (*Junges Europa. Szenarien des Umbruchs*) in 2013. Within the pages of this latter book, the two authors lay out six future scenarios in which radical change might occur. Their illustrations show in concrete terms exactly how social turmoil can lead to transformations in the direction of patriotism, all while dismissing the usual dogmas and platitudes of the German Right. They draw on the concept of "Young Europe" (*Giovine Europa*), coined in 1834 by the Italian revolutionary Giuseppe Mazzini, who in turn was inspired by the secret society of the same name. In contrast to many representatives of the liberal Right, the authors advocate for a united and federal Europe. Their idea of Europe is at odds with that of the European Union, whose centralism and elitism they reject, instead calling for an European state constituted from below by a popular plebiscite. This projected future development is set against the background of the protest movements of Podemos in Spain and *Manif pour tous* in France.

It is remarkable just how extensively Stein and Menzel think outside the German box, looking especially towards Southern Europe, where political phenomena such as left-wing populist protest movements and countercultural projects of the neo-fascist right-wing such as Casa Pound have piqued their interest. Particularly intriguing is their focus on the ideas of the life-reform (*Lebensreform*) movement that is otherwise particularly dominant on the Left. Here, they adopt economic ideas from the French discourse of "*Décroissance*," a term which can be roughly translated into English as "degrowth." In contrast to the capitalistic economic model, which demands constant growth in order to maintain the material prosperity that it has generated, *Décroissance* takes a diametrically opposite approach. Through a voluntary renunciation of luxury, growth is to be abandoned. This reduction in economic growth is to be done for the sake of a deceleration of life, a movement towards sustainable economic activity, the protection of nature, and a modest way of being. The movement is not only aimed at striking a nerve in the upper middle class but, because of its "limiting" character, functions in a downright reactionary fashion in the face of a=the globalized and networked world. Its radicalism lies in the fact that it does not simply demand a reform of the capitalist, consumerist society, but its end.[1]

It is important that this not become a broad political movement, but rather that it remain a current of social activism, suggesting a grassroots alternative to everything wrong with society. For this reason, it initially strives for changes in consumption at the individual and local levels, from neighborhood gatherings, ride-sharing, and local bartering markets to the unmonetized exchange of goods and services in private life. The most successful manifestation of *Décroissance* to date is the Transition Town movement proposed by Iren Rob Hopkins in 2006, which attempts to prepare humanity for a post-fossil future and a sustainable economic model by strengthening

---

1   Philip Stein and Felix Menzel, *Junges Europa. Szenarien des Umbruchs* (BN Anstoß II, 2013), 57–59.

local and regional economic circuits and promoting reduced fuel consumption in rural communities. By 2013, this environmental and sustainable development initiative had sprouted up in over 300 major cities worldwide.[2]

This grassroots approach, which is central to Stein's thinking, can also be observed in the citizen's "One Percent for Our Country" (*Ein Prozent für unser Land*) initiative, presented to the public in 2015 by Götz Kubitschek, which is based on a simple and powerful idea: it would only take one percent of all existing Germans, i.e., 800,000 men, to create a powerful political advocacy group capable of precipitating political change in Germany.[3] The aim of this political initiative is the restoration and protection of the German legal system. By this, Kubitschek intends the following: (1) securing the border against illegal immigration, (2) the registration and systematic deportation of all illegal immigrants, and (3) the protection of people and private property. It was towards these ends that the resistance against Merkel's government began to organize and network in the wake of the first major successes of PEGIDA and the AfD. The organization connects individuals with civic groups that organize demonstrations and protests against the out-of-touch German political class. A second important activity that the organization has pursued is the (financial) support of patriots who have landed in dire straits brought about by Antifa or other globalist groups. In the interest of building a counterculture, patriotic house projects such as the Mühle Cottbus or the Flammberg center in Halle have offered their support. In addition, journalists contributing to the project conduct research and provide insight into events which would otherwise be left solely in hands of the one-sided liberal media apparatus in the country. A camera team from *EinProzent* was in Paris at the end of 2018, on site for the protests of the Yellow Vests against the anti-popular and globalist politics

---

2   Ibid., 61–62.

3   *„Ein Prozent". Eine kleine Projektübersicht* [https://www.einprozent.de/blog/intern/ein-prozent-eine-kleine-projektuebersicht/2436].

of President Macron. The association's social commitment is also expressed in their support for the local homeless of Dresden and the establishment of alternative unions. Since election fraud in Germany occurs frequently, the association has also been involved in monitoring elections since 2016, and have detected irregularities. This has created a larger political mandate for the AfD. Furthermore, in view of the rising violence against Germans instigated by foreigners, the association organizes legal support for those affected, as was the case in the murder of Marcus H. from Wittenberg, as well as the situation involving four Germans displaying civil courage as they defended fellow citizens from a rampaging Iraqi in 2017.

In 2016, Stein founded the Jungeuropa Publishing House, which has translated and republished the forerunners and direct representatives of the *Nouvelle Droite*, such as Alain de Benoist and Dominique Venner, historical authors of Eurofascism like Pierre Drieu la Rochelle and Robert Brasillach, and socialists such as Hermann Heller. Its new releases also include the controversially received anthology *Marx from the Right* and the polemical pamphlet *Aristocracy* by Wolfgang Bended. What differentiates Jungeuropa from other right-wing publishing houses in Germany is that it draws on and disseminates ideas specifically from the French *Nouvelle Droite*. As with its Gallic forebears, it does not shy away from engaging with leftist thinkers or disseminating the potentially scandalous historical writings of Eurofascism. Stein also takes a critical view of his own camp concerning its political theory. On that count, he writes in his preface to *Marx from the Right* that many people on his side of the barricades have been deceived by the masquerade of liberalism and capitalism, which are seen as the only option. Liberalism (on the ideological level) and capitalism (on the economic level) have subtly established themselves in the Westerners' minds as seemingly rational ideologies. The consequence of this process is that both seem inevitable, and a world far removed from the logic of the market is no longer conceivable. Therefore, Stein argues, the conflict over capitalism in the right-wing camp is representative of something entirely different. For him, it is about whether the Right is ready for a new beginning and an intellectual overcoming of capitalism and liberalism as ideologies of separation, or whether it only wishes to reform the currently established system. A compromise between the two camps is not possible, because this would nullify any hope of resurrecting community. According to de Benoist, the conjoined twins of liberalism and capitalism inevitably result in an ideology of isolation and, thus, the end of every organic community.[4]

Stein argues that the importance of engaging with Marx for the anti-capitalist Right lies above all in the possibility of union with the Left. The exact form such a union would take must first be elaborated by a young Right that manages to address any problem without any self-imposed prohibition in thought. Dispassionate readings of Marx could thus put a stop to the profiteers of exploitation on the one hand and, on the other, could help avoid falling into the binary class struggle of Marxist ideology. This new engagement with Marx lays the groundwork for a new theory and praxis which is alone capable of unifying the Right, Stein concludes.[5] He supports that faction of the German Right which takes its cues from the French New Right while trying to find a new impetus for change. One of the most interesting aspects of this faction is its grassroots approach to politics, which works alongside One Percent to aid local and regional patriotic initiatives. Theoretically, through his engagement with socialism and (Euro-)fascism, Stein also seeks to develop a non-dogmatic approach to European intellectual history — something otherwise forbidden to the vacillators and liberals of the German Right. The only obstacle to such a leap is the residual malaise of (post-)modernity in the political sphere.

---

4   Stein 2018, 9–10.

5   Ibid., 11–12.

Right-Wing Anti-Capitalism: Marx Viewed from the Right

IN THE popular political perception, there are seldom two terms as mutually incompatible as "right-wing" and "anti-capitalism." Anyone who even utters the name of Karl Marx is almost certain to be ostracized on the Right. This is exactly what happened in 2018 when Jungeuropa published the anthology *Marx Viewed from the Right* on the 200th birthday of the intellectual father of communism. But why should one engage with the theories of Karl Marx more than 35 years after the collapse of the USSR? For one thing, because liberalism, the former ideological adversary of communism, is still alive, and its neoliberal variations are also very popular on the 'liberal Right' (such as the American neoconservatives). Secondly, because the reception of left-wing concepts on the Right is one of the main features of the New Right, apart from which it is otherwise typical for the Right to defend capitalism and neoliberalism at any cost.

In this context, the political scientist Benedikt Kaiser states that many right-wing groups are misled by the myth that neoliberalism is not ideological. They suffer from a mental block which leads them to reject any critique of capitalism as "left-wing" or "communist."[1] And yet, this has not always been the case with the Right. In fact, the contrary was true for a long time: right-wing critics of capitalism already existed in the 19th century, such as Karl Rodbertus (1805–1875), who advocated for a "socialism from above" (*Sozialismus von oben*).

---

1 Benedikt Kaiser, " " in *Marx von Rechts* (Dresden: Jungeuropa, 2018), 15.

Adolph Wagner (1835–1917) contradicted the "British-liberal concept of man as an egoistic, materialistic being" by asserting that man is not moldable.[2] According to Kaiser, the anti-capitalistic Right experienced its apogee in Germany during the Weimar Republic. The national-revolutionary current of the Conservative Revolution brought about, among others, the magazine *Resistance* [*Widerstand*], headed by Ernst Niekisch (1889–1967) who, also directing the journal *Action* [*Die Tat*], was the primary critic of capitalism in his time. Within the NSDAP, Otto Strasser (1897–1974) was equally critical of capitalism before ultimately being forced to leave Germany due to his opposition to Adolf Hitler. Strasser continued to publish until his death in 1974, but he failed to achieve a theoretical depth and clarity in his critique of capitalism that would be comparable to that of the Marxist critique.

The shift towards centrist politics on the German Right and the unreserved endorsement of capitalism occurred after the Second World War, in the 1950s-60s, through the "integration with the West" [*Westbindung*] influenced by the United States. Since then, those factions of the Right which are critically positioned against the United States, capitalism, and liberalism have been subjected to a miserable existence. This only changed with the emergence of a new right-wing tendency around Henning Eichberg, Wolfgang Strauss, and Lothar Penz in the 1970s.[3] This ethnopluralist right-wing, highly critical of capitalism, existed until the 1980s. Its magazine, *We Ourselves* (*Wir selbst*, 1979–2002), advocated popular instead of party rule, a human economy as an antithesis to neoliberalism and the mania of privatization, a holistic ecology, and a newfound emphasis on regionalistic approaches.[4] The anti-capitalistic Right finally received a more favorable response in France, where both the national-revolutionary

---

2   Ibid., 18.

3   Ibid., 26.

4   Ibid., 28–29.

ideas of the Conservative Revolution and the ideas of Henning Eichberg enjoyed a greater reception than in Germany. Thus, the *Nouvelle Droite* in France developed very differently from the right-wing camp in Germany which, while in the sphere of influence of its flagship, *Junge Freiheit*, remained unfailingly "old-school nationalist" and restorative, which is to say that it remained loyal to the Old Right. In Alain de Benoist's thought, the struggle against liberalism is aimed at three main pillars: capitalism, human rights, and the market economy. De Benoist explains the Right's hard stance on this line of thought as the result of economic liberalism being historically more right-wing, while social liberalism found its home on the Left.[5]

The Right's reception of Marx is therefore expedient, Kaiser argues, precisely because the Left today has made peace with capitalism and withdrawn into the cultural sphere following "the total emancipation of the '68ers." From this position, it has set the tone until this very day. Far from calling for a right-wing "cultural Marxism," Kaiser calls for a reevaluation of Marx's actual thought. In many respects, *Das Kapital* is still relevant today, Kaiser argues, because capitalism must commodify everything and transform whatever it can into alienated value. This also includes the term "industrial reserve army" in relation to mass-immigration and digitalization, as well as a new reassessment of the base/superstructure model and Marx's thesis on the preservation (*Bewahrung*) of social forms.[6] Kaiser argues that through critiquing capitalism through the lens of Marx's writings, it is possible to overcome the dichotomy of liberalism and the eventual totalitarianism which develops to ensure liberal supremacy. To paraphrase de Benoist, we must fight against the main enemy, which takes the form of capitalism and the consumer society on the economic level, the individual on philosophical level, the bourgeoisie on the societal level, and the United States on the geopolitical level. These

---

5   Ibid., 31.

6   Ibid., 57.

various manifestations need to be fought in order to save democracy from the clutches of international finance.[7]

In his articles "Karl Marx and Commodity Fetishism" and "Value Criticism," de Benoist exhaustively questions Marx's thought, asking what in it might be of use to today's Right. One major difficulty in answering this question is how little Marx has actually been read, particularly since the majority of his writings were only published posthumously. This is not least due to the communist movement itself, especially its developments under Lenin and Stalin, who were interested in molding Marx's thought into an official ideology, forging it into a shape beneficial to their aims.[8] De Benoist differentiates in the first instance, following Robert Kunze, between the esoteric and the exoteric Marx. Whereas the exoteric (directed outwardly) Marx is the author of *The Communist Manifesto*, the esoteric (inward-looking) Marx is the author of *Capital*. For de Benoist, it is not Marx the revolutionary theorist who is of interest, but rather the exoteric side of his work which deals with the social forms of human life that are important for capitalism: labor, commodities, value, money.

In the field of critique, de Benoist first revises Karl Marx's idea of the inevitability of communist revolution, which he considers to be the weakest part of the German's theory, misconstruing as it does the flexible character of capitalism. De Benoist also rejects Marx's teleological thinking, the product of the 19th century's obsession with progress.[9] In order to better understand Marx's thought, one must first bear in mind that he understands capital as social relation, not as an object. His critique of capital does not stop at the economic dimension of capitalism, as is the case with the present Left, but also critiques the social and cultural side of liberalism. For this reason, Marx (like de Benoist) is a staunch opponent of human rights, due to their

---

7　Ibid., 63.

8　Alain de Benoist, " " in *Marx von Rechts,*, 65–66.

9　Ibid., 68.

foundation on the idea of an abstract individual subject. Because human rights only protect the individual and, by extension, its economic potential, such thinking must be resisted. Viewed through the lens of human rights, only the *homo oeconomicus* is human — any people who wish to assert their collective ties are inhuman in comparison. It is thus not the citizen who is duty-bound to the state in belonging to its human community, but only the individual who is torn from all collective ties. The only sense in which the individual still interacts with other humans is in his economic transactions. In this way, the liberal human being is reduced to his economic function. From the point of view of Marxian criticism, this view is completely erroneous, for it is rather the case that man is a social being by nature, and he can exist only through and in social relationships.[10]

One of the most important concepts in Marx's thought is class. This is tied to historical development and its phases of production, whereby Marxian thought assumes an inevitable development *via* class struggle towards a classless society. Marx's analysis of capitalism is predicated on the worker not selling his labor, but his manpower. Exploitation in the capitalist economy derives from its creation of goods that are sold for more than they are worth. The entrepreneur ultimately appropriates the surplus value, wherein the contradiction of wage labor emerges. Marx adopts the distinction already made by Aristotle between natural economy and money-making, and now speaks of exchange value and use value. While use value satisfies a private need, exchange value ensures that all goods are sold or bought. The use value serves to cover human needs; the exchange value allows human needs to devolve into money. Thus, all concrete work is converted into abstract work.[11]

This is exactly where the esoteric Marx comes in to accuse liberalism of having replaced earlier dependences by creating new, abstract

---

10   Ibid., 69.

11   Ibid., 70–71.

relationships of dependency which are imposed on allegedly free and equal individuals through the laws of value that assume the form of practical constraint. Marx recognizes here that capitalism underpins itself with labor and fetishized social conditions, going beyond mere class struggle.[12] In Marxian theory, the substance of the commodity is the labor which produced it. This exists in an objectified form and represents a socio-historical world of ideas associated with certain social practices. The dual nature of goods is of crucial importance: the nature of the commodity consists in it being, on one hand, a concrete thing with its own attributes while, on the other hand, representing a purely quantitative and abstract value. With the modern age, the dual nature of goods took on a new meaning: use value was replaced by exchange value.

Capitalism privileges exchange, and the globalization of this exchange only becomes possible when the human has gradually lost the means of his own production. Exchange value (the value gained in the course of exchanging something) is determined by a purely abstract and universal set of principles. The resultant market price is unrelated to the item's unique, unquantifiable attributes. The exchange value is precisely such a value, as it relates only to the amount of money corresponding to the commodity's price. In this state of affairs, whenever one produces a good for the market, its value is universally exchangeable with all other values.[13] The objective of capitalism is to convert all things into this abstract value. As its ultimate consequence, exchange value creates in man a quasi-religious relationship with the products he consumes. This is what Marx calls the fetish character of goods. It is here that the anonymous character of capitalism reveals itself in conditioning all human relationships by the exchange of goods and the laws of the market.[14] This fetishism is

---

12   Ibid., 82.

13   Ibid., 83.

14   Ibid., 84.

ultimately laid bare in the natural character we now assign to labor and commodities. In this paradigm, objects come to have their own life, which leads to an inversion in the relationship between subject and object.

Man no longer rules over things. Rather, things rule people. According to Marx, one should not make the mistake of understanding this as merely the rule of one class. Goods and capital form a common system, which increasingly impacts the behavior of people even while lacking any specific owners. Capitalism is, moreover, a subject-less process which results in a permanent self-valorization of value. Capitalism does not aim for the satisfaction of needs, but solely for the perpetuation of exchange, so that any sum of money turns into an even greater sum of money. Beyond that, it is also marked by a qualitative break, since labor ceases to be a means and becomes an end in itself as a production activity. The task of labor lies in creating products which take the form of goods. In this regard, capitalism marks a break with all other forms of historical life. Like goods, labor also holds a dual character. Concrete labor creates a use value, abstract labor an exchange value, whereby there are two aspects of every instance of labor. The first form denotes the goods actually produced, while the second alludes to the self-mediating form of social relationships. Since abstract labor can only be estimated quantitatively, it requires a uniform and homogenous kind of time, for which peculiarities and people are unimportant.[15] In its mania for productivity, it finally tends to self-destruction, as it wishes to produce increasingly more goods in ever shorter periods of time, making the expenditure of human energy an end in itself all the while as labor is made increasingly superfluous.[16]

Following Moishe Postone's critique of value, Alain de Benoist ascertains that the fight against capitalism is not a war between workers

---

15   Ibid., 88.

16   Ibid., 90.

and the bourgeoisie, but between people and value. In its dreams of limitlessness, capital tries to free itself from all materiality and thus ultimately from the planet and its inhabitants.[17] Only when man leaves behind the ontology of work and value, which drive him into a war of all against all and subordinate him to the de-personalizing rule of cold calculation, can society be liberated from capitalism.[18]

17   Ibid., 93.
18   Ibid., 94.

The Globalization of Anti-Globalism: Arktos and the New Right in Scandinavia and Beyond

ARKTOS FIGURES among the largest publishing houses responsible for popularizing the works of the New Right. Since its founding in 2009 at a meeting between four members of the Scandinavian national-revolutionary think tank Motpol in Aarhus, Denmark, Arktos has released more than 300 titles in 16 languages. In its early days, in order to be able to work efficiently with as low a budget as possible, Arktos co-founder Daniel Friberg moved the publishing house to India, where seeking solutions to problems such as Internet outages became part of a real adventure.[1] The efforts devoted to this great project of the New Right in Sweden and beyond eventually began to pay off, enabling the publishing house to transfer its operations to Europe in 2015. Among Arktos' greatest merits are the first English translation of Alexander Dugin's *Fourth Political Theory* and the translation and popularization of Alain de Benoist as well as the New Right dissident Guillaume Faye. Arktos has also translated and published authors of the German Conservative Revolution, representatives of radical ecology, such as Pentti Linkola,[2] Indian authors such as Porus Hami Havewala, and representatives of the

---

1   Daniel Friberg, *Die Rückkehr der Echten Rechten. Handbuch für die wahre Opposition* (London: Arktos, 2015). English edition: *The Real Right Returns: A Handbook for the True Opposition* (London: Arktos, 2015; revised and expanded edition 2024).

2   Pentti Linkola, *Can Life Prevail?* (Arktos, 2011).

American and European Dissident Right, as well as prominent paleoconservatives, such as Paul Gottfried, Stephen Baskerville, and William S. Lind.

As illustrated in the publisher's mission statement, Arktos' motto for its publishing is "Making Anti-Globalism Global," which means not siding with any particular current on the Right, nor with any specific religion or worldview. In general, the publishing house aims to present individuals and views ignored by the mainstream Western media, while simultaneously offering alternative perspectives to the prevailing culture. Since its inception, Arktos has operated in the interest of making the New Right accessible to wider audiences. According to early Arktos editor John Morgan, since the concept of the "New Right" has so many meanings, the publisher has also opted to use the term "true Right," originally coined by Julius Evola.[3] By this they mean a Right that seeks to restore the values and ideals which were in currency in Europe before the advent of liberalism. The "true Right" derives its revolutionary content precisely from its positive relation to Europe's pre-liberal past, such as the Holy Roman Empire and the democracy of ancient Athens, in order to grasp the autonomy, freedom, and diversity present in those times, and to draw on such as inspiration for a better future. Thus, there are revolutionary ideas to be revealed through looking into the past, into the world before liberalism.[4]

Why did Swedes decide to import the New Right from France? As Joakim Andersen (co-editor of Motpol) has explained, it all began with a desire to break out of the impasse into which the Swedish

---

3   See John Morgan, "Forging the True Right," preface to Friberg, *The Real Right Returns*. This perception likely stems from the extensive catalogue of Arktos itself, which has translated not only the intellectual forefathers of the New Right and the New Right's leading thinkers themselves, but also the movement's dissidents (many of whom ultimately tended towards becoming right-wing liberal) such as Guillaume Faye.

4   Morgan, "Forging the True Right," preface to Friberg, *The Real Right Returns*, ix.

Right had maneuvered itself by 2005. Only a conservative Right existed in Sweden at that time, one that levelled only a moderate critique of mass immigration and represented a nationalistic right-wing continuation of the Old Right. An authentic, consistent Right, one with strong ideas that had not been adapted to accommodate left-wing liberalism, had yet to arise.[5] Hence, the primary task of the "true Right" consisted in showing Swedes that they have a culture of their own, that they are European, and, as such, have a history as well as legitimate claims to their inheritance. Thus, in Andersen's words: "The solution to the problem of breaking the Swedish impasse, it was suggested, is to introduce and adapt the school of thought which is known as the European New Right."[6] In this context, Andersen indicated, it was also necessary to oppose the false "right-wing." By "false right-wing," Andersen means those "right-wing" forces which are only presented as Right by the media, but which are defined solely by "rhetorical focus on 'the market', its fixation on 'individualism' and 'freedom', its Atlanticist loyalty to Brussels and the White House, and its apathy or hostility towards any conception of European identities, values, and traditions."[7] One example of this is Sweden's parliamentary right-wing, to which Andersen refers as the "imposter Right." He reiterates this demand for a dissociation from the "false Right" by arguing that the ideas of 1789 (meaning the Enlightenment as a whole) must be replaced by the ideas of the New Right. In this view, the New Right offers a comprehensive alternative worldview, encompassing anthropology, social ideas, and historiography.

A brief and concise presentation of the program of the Scandinavian New Right can be found in the 2015 volume *The Real Right Returns: A Handbook for the True Opposition*, penned by Daniel Friberg. In this book, conceived as an introduction to the New Right

---

5   Joakim Andersen, "Daniel Friberg and the Swedish Right," foreword to Friberg, *The Real Right Returns*, xiii.

6   Ibid., xiv.

7   Ibid., xv.

and as a handbook for activists, Friberg presents a critique of the "false Right" and its eternal rear-guard action against the strange alliance of globalist left-wing liberals and right-wingers with an affinity for capitalism. According to Friberg, this union has facilitated the demise of Europe. In this darkest hour, in which everything seems lost, the true Right, like "men among the ruins," must oppose the demise of Europe and prepare for a rebirth of the continent. This undertaking is fraught with difficulty, since liberal consumer society has already devastated regional and national identities. Salvation does not lie in parliamentarism, but in metapolitics, whose developments might end up being carried out through party politics only in an ideal scenario. To this end, what is needed is a struggle for cultural power, following Alain de Benoist's concept of a cultural revolution from the Right, which understands metapolitics as a war for social change at the level of culture, worldview, and thought.[8] According to Friberg, a political elite which does not engage in the metapolitical struggle cannot bring about lasting change. Therefore, the Right must recognize the need for metapolitical work and declare the formation of a metapolitical vanguard as the main task of the New Right in Europe.[9]

With regard to political orientation points, Friberg formulates the following guidelines: the real Right should commit to long-term, principled thinking. This means being geared towards providing an answer to the question of authentic identity which vindicates a people, its language, and its culture. This vision is set in contrast to contemporary Western society, which constructs identity via media-induced impulses, sexual orientation, and artificial needs.[10] As Friberg concludes, the end of the modern age shows that the formation of identity *via* individualism and socialist class analysis has

---

8   Friberg, *The Real Right Returns*, 21.

9   Ibid., 22.

10   Ibid., 23.

failed. Instead, ethnic identity has proved to be the natural starting point for identity formation.[11]

On the geopolitical level, Europe must end its subordination to the United States and pursue its own interests. In doing so, Friberg argues, the EU should not be further centralized; instead, regional and national identities should be protected under the auspices of a larger framework, which might bear the name *"Imperium Europa"* or "European Federation." Friberg sees security issues, trade, and foreign policy as the only areas in which bureaucratic centralization can be tolerated.[12]

In the economic sphere, the primacy of politics should be reinstated. On this point, Friberg is primarily concerned with fighting the oligarchization of the economy. In the future, power should be openly exercised by people who can answer for their actions. Ultimately, the harmful influence of private money on politics must be curbed, and representatives of the European nations who are determined to fight for this should be advanced into positions of power. Friberg emphasizes that the primacy of politics over the economy does not mean regulation or planning. Instead, it means fighting against the neoliberal, therapeutic state (Gottfried) which regulates the life of its citizens down to the smallest detail; moreover, it means not leaving the organization of social welfare to the markets. In the future, social assistance should be restricted to Europeans in order to curb mass immigration into the Old World.[13] The aim of this economic development should be a society with a market, not an international market economy. It is important to cleanse large social domains of economic influence, such as religion, culture, and even sports associations.

In the interest of ethnopluralism, the new Europe must commit to Europe as the subject of politics — one that stands up for its own

---

11   Ibid., 24.

12   Ibid., 25.

13   Ibid., 26.

interests and those of its peoples. This, of course, does not exclude goodwill for and cooperation with other peoples, but the politicians who represent Europe must under no circumstances take abstract humanity and human rights as their point of reference. Instead of imperialism under the pretexts of human rights and regime-change wars, diplomacy should once again be oriented towards political realism.[14] Friberg calls not only for an end to Western interference in the affairs of other peoples, but also for an end to mass immigration to Europe and a restriction of Americanization. With regard to parliamentarianism, he does not assign it a central role, as can be seen from his remarks on metapolitics, but views it as the result of broader cultural and political planning. Friberg regards political violence as senseless, since it would only cause unprecedented devastation, as the revolutions of past centuries have shown. Despite these obstacles, Friberg is convinced that the victory of the New Right in Europe is only a question of time.[15]

One particularly interesting chapter in Friberg's book is titled "Brief Advice on Gender Roles," in which the author manages to thematize the issue of gender roles without discrediting himself before his right-wing audience accustomed to associating such discourse with the postmodern Left. Friberg states in the introduction that most men and women in Sweden are nothing to be proud of. The average Westerner is cowardly, timid, and conformist, having lost his honor and dignity. The degeneration of contemporary society manifests itself through distortions in gender, and it becomes fundamentally difficult to lead a life of integrity in the modern world, since it attacks every form of honor, virtue, and propriety.[16] In his appeal to men, Friberg demands a return to real masculinity. More precisely, he calls for a return to the assertive masculinity, for abandoning the

---

14   Ibid., 27–28.

15   Ibid., 29–31.

16   Ibid., 53.

notion of equality between the sexes, as well as for turning away from hedonism and the pursuit of a partner. Instead, the best way to serve Europe is for a man to spend his time on personal development and professional advancement.

When it comes to the role of women in politics and the question of quotas, Friberg begs us to keep in mind that women, in general, are underrepresented in political movements besides feminism. The few women who dedicate themselves to the cause should therefore be valued, but not placed on a pedestal.[17] With respect to the family, he recommends that men take the lead. Ultimately, the overriding principle must be to bring as many children into the world as possible. Regarding a man's circle of friends, Friberg advises the reader to follow the model of a *Männerbund*, ordered by laws of honor. In such a case, rivalry over women is to be taboo, while other men's daughters and ex-girlfriends are off limits, sowing as these do the seeds of discord between men.[18] In his advice to women, Friberg warns that they are the main target of the politics of guilt, multicultural propaganda, and the idea of equality. By voluntarily being part of the thought police in everyday life, much more often than men, they play a central role in maintaining the present order. He therefore advises them to "get their priorities straight." Instead of aspiring to a career in a multinational company, he recommends bringing at least three children into the world, arguing that, in a woman's twilight years, her fulfillment as a woman derived from her offspring is incomparably greater than that which she gets from life-long service in a career, which counts for little after retirement.[19] Women should leave the sexual revolution behind and observe more restraint, for only then does falling in love become possible. Furthermore, they should not adopt male behavior, but cultivate their own femininity. Only the

17   Ibid., 58.

18   Ibid., 59.

19   Ibid., 60.

enforcement of specific gender roles enables them to become part of "the vanguard in the reformation of European society, and the restoration of our ancient, traditional ideals."[20] These ideals, Friberg writes, "once built the great civilisation of Europe, and they will re-build it when this age of darkness ends."[21]

Overall, Friberg's "handbook for the true opposition" offers not only insight into the Scandinavian Right, but also a good guide for aspiring activists. He emphasizes the importance of cultural strug-gle and metapolitics, and rejects the belief that party politics is the central or even only form of politics. Thus, Friberg addresses the important fact that "imposter right-wingers" — the majority of the European Right — remain shackled to the *idée fixe* of liberalism, fet-ishizing any party that appears to be right-wing when it is, in fact, right-liberal.

---

20 Ibid., 61.

21 Ibid.

The French New Right Today: From GRECE to the Iliade Institute and Strategika

S INCE THE birth of the *Nouvelle Droite* in France in the Spring of 1968, the New Right has not only spread throughout Europe, but has also developed further in its own homeland. The publishing organs established by Alain de Benoist still carry on today. In terms of their functionality, they all cover a certain field. While *Nouvelle École* fulfills the function of a theoretical journal, *Éléments* is conceived as a daily magazine, and *Krisis* is dedicated to cultivating dialogue between left-wing and right-wing authors. Another institute associated with the New Right is the *Institut Iliade*, founded in 2014 in memory of Dominique Venner. Its coat of arms brandishes the Owl of Minerva perched on a sword, which embodies the triad of nature, aesthetics, and the elite. The stated goal of the Institute is to oppose the Great Replacement, defend European civilization, and bring into relief the peculiarities and the richness of the common European cultural heritage, which is to be resurrected through a "reawakening of European consciousness."[1] These cultural roots of European identity are formulated through conferences, publications, and cultural events. The Institute's conferences mainly focus on the topics of immigration, demographic replacement, and European identity, as well as the aesthetic-cultural ideal and the need for an ecology from the Right.

---

1   See: *Guardians of Heritage: The Iliade Institute's Call to Action* (London: Arktos, 2024); *For a European Awakening: Nature, Excellence, Beauty* (London: Arktos, 2023).

In the field of geopolitics, a new institute emerged in 2020: the think tank Strategika. Led by political analyst and geopolitical expert Pierre-Antoine Plaquevent, the institute is joined by historians Youssef Hindi and Pierr Le Vigan. In its geopolitical analysis, Strategika focuses not only on political actors and international relations, but also on interdisciplinary collaborations as represented by the novel field of theopolitics (the coordinated study of theology and geopolitics). In his essay "Multipolarity and the Open Society: Geopolitical Realism vs. Cosmopolitical Utopia," Plaquevent delivers a remarkable analysis of the current geopolitical situation and offers insight into the differences between the ideas of the New Right on the one hand, and those of the neo-Western movement around US President Donald Trump and the populist movements influenced by him on the other hand.[2] Plaquevent assumes that there are two competing political currents within Western liberalism. First, there are the globalists, represented among others by George Soros and his Open Society Foundation, as well as by the ruling elites of the European Union. Their stated goal is the total anthropological transformation of man and the dissolution of nation-states into a single world government. The idea of the Open Society, first formulated by Karl Popper, is that all of humanity should be merged in a single world superstate. As Plaquevent sees it, the Open Society is the result of the secularization process that began in Europe with the Renaissance. In this understanding, the anti-Stalinist ideas of Freudo-Marxism are combined with Karl Popper's liberal critique of authoritarianism and historicism. Instead of assuming that historical processes are clearly determined by predictable social laws, the advocates of the Open Society assume that the entire world is inevitably developing towards an End of History, and that all peoples

---

2   Pierre-Antoine Plaquevent, "Multipolarity and the Open Society: Geopolitical Realism vs. Cosmopolitical Utopia," *Strategika* (9 February 2020) [https:// strategika.fr/2020/02/09/multipolarity-and-open-society-geopolitical-realism-versus-cosmopolitical-utopia-pluriversum-vs-universum/].

are destined to form into a single *demos*. The "universe" critiqued in Schmitt's *Concept of the Political* can also be recognized in this development as a process whose trajectory is the erasure of diversity, of the *pluriversum,* in order to achieve world peace.

Since the Political can only exist in diversity, the ultimate goal of the Open Society is a cosmopolitan world society, the ultimate consequence of which is the end of politics and therefore geopolitics. In the course of this change, the Open Society dissolves the international order and decomposes it from within by employing supranational and transnational identities, which ultimately spark global civil war, as witnessed in the regime change wars initiated by the United States in Afghanistan, Iraq, Syria, Egypt, Ukraine, and Hong Kong. In opposition to this faction stand the partisans and pirates of an increasingly fluid social order (see Carl Schmitt's antithesis between land and sea), fighting each other in ever more asymmetrical and unconventional conflicts. In the globalist view, these conflicts constitute necessary wars leading to an end of international antagonism and thus the end of history. At the end of cosmopolitanism, with its expectation of salvation from the state, stands not a peaceful order, but a world government enforced through behavioral control and violence, analogous to the early communist states. After nation-states, a "World Leviathan" would thus emerge, whose brutality is unpredictable and untamed. With reference to the Yellow Vest protests of 2020, Plaquevent indicates that the liberal Leviathan protects the immigrants it needs as slaves to dissolve nation-states, while gouging out the eyes of the protesting French. The Macron-Merkel Leviathan was, in its time, the blueprint for the entire West.

On the other side of this conflict, Plaquevent sees conservatives who are labelled neo-Westerners, such as Donald Trump, Viktor Orban, and Matteo Salvini. The neo-Western trend in international relations defines itself in terms of reinforcing the Anglo-Protestant world and the US alliance with Europe and Israel along with rejecting international institutions and norms. In the sense of the clash of cultures, the neo-Westerners invoke the fight against terrorism, which they exclusively identify with Islam, whether Sunni or Shia. At the same time, they seek to prevent a strategic alliance in Eurasia not only between Europe and Russia, but also between Moscow and Beijing. For a free hand in the economic war between the US-led West and the Eurasian partnership between Russia and China, the new-Westerners want to limit the influence of George Soros's networks outside Western civilization. To achieve this, they seek to cordon off the geopolitical coastal countries, i.e., the edges of the Eurasian peninsula which border Russia and China's spheres of influence. The undermining of these two Eurasian powers is to be accomplished via fomenting pro-Western uprisings and coups.

While the neoconservatives emerged as the dominant current of right-wing liberalism and constantly advocate direct military intervention and unilateral action against "rogue nations," the neo-Westerners act more pragmatically and de-emphasize ideological commitments, as can be seen from Trump's dismissal of the neocon John Bolton, or the US occupation of Syria's oil fields. An example of this conflict between the two geopolitical currents in the West can be observed in the Israeli-American establishment in the wake of the Epstein affair. While the globalist left-wing surrounding Hillary Clinton, Bill Clinton, and Israeli ex-Prime Minister Ehud Barak maintained their contacts with Epstein, it was the neo-Westerner and right-wing philo-Zionist Trump who supported Bradley Edwards, the legal counsel for Epstein's victims. The fact that Ehud Barak visited Epstein's villa in New York with his face covered after the first allegations of abuse became known sparked a scandal in Israel, ultimately helping Benjamin Netanyahu win election in the Knesset. During the Brexit campaign, the Brexit camp was backed by Trump, while supporters of remaining in the EU were buttressed by the Euro-globalists associated with George Soros.

Likewise, these two Western camps irreconcilably oppose each other on the subjects of abortion, national identity, LGBTQ+

rights, and co-existence (in the sense of integration/assimilation vs. Multiculturalism). In this context, the neoconservative Daniel Pipes even speaks of a fundamental conflict between Judaism in the diaspora and that in Israel, whereby he assumes that the majority of Jews in Europe are left-wing liberal and globalist-minded, while the majority in Israel are right-wing liberal Zionists. Accordingly, Pipes accuses the Jews in the diaspora of opposing an alliance with right-wing populists aimed at strengthening conservatism, which would permit the Right to oppose the "true enemies of the West: the Left and Islam." Consequently, propagandists pursuing this objective such as Eric Zemmour and Ivan Rioufol employ a strategy aimed at steering the European states opposing globalism of the Soros kind into a Jewish-Western alliance with its core in the United States. This geopolitical school of thought dates back to Robert Strausz-Hupé, who founded the Foreign Policy Research Institute (FPRI) in the 1950s to intellectually arm the US during the Cold War. This ideological father of neoconservatism postulated the theory that the United States must save Europe from the claws of China, Russia, and Arab Asia. These ideas were eventually adopted by the neoconservative think tank Project for the New American Century (PNAC). However, while the neoconservatives still wish to expand their power across the globe, the neo-Westerners are mainly concerned with preventing the American Empire from disintegrating under the weight of its internal contradictions.

This "pan-conservatism," developed further by Samuel Huntington, has registered many victories in the West, although it has recently begun to suffer setbacks with the Strache scandal (the "Ibiza affair") in Austria, the collapse of the coalition between Lega Nord and the Five Star Movement in Italy, and repeated delays of Brexit. According to Plaquevent, this demonstrates the persistent power of the globalists around Soros. Europe's future prospects, either with the globalists or with the neo-Westernists, are not particularly rosy. Whereas a victory for the Soros side would usher in the globalist government and spell the end for the nations, a neo-Western victory would be unacceptable for Europe, given its geopolitical interests in the Middle East and Eurasia. Even a Eurasian order dominated solely by China — an increasingly likely outcome — is undesirable for Europe, since it would degrade the latter to the status of Chinese satellite. Instead, Plaquevent advocates a fourth geostrategic orientation of Europe: cooperation with Russia along the Paris-Berlin-Moscow axis. This would be a strategic continental agreement between non-aligned sovereigns capable of ending American influence on the continent and preventing a takeover by Beijing.

Felix Menzel and Benedikt Kaiser: Media Icons and Looking towards the Left

AMONG THE German representatives of the New Right, Benedikt Kaiser and Felix Menzel deserve special attention for their projects, international networking, and editorial work as part of *Sezession* magazine. Born in 1987, Kaiser studied political science at university and wrote his master's thesis on "Concepts of Europe and Social Critique in the Thinking of the Eurofascist Pierre Drieu de la Rochelle." Since 2020, he has worked as an editor for the Antaios publishing house and as a German-language correspondent for the French *Nouvelle Droite's* magazine *Éléments*. In addition to his deep knowledge of Eurofascist currents, he has co-authored a book with Eric Fröhlich entitled *The Phenomenon of Island Fascism: Blackshirts, Blueshirts, and Other Authoritarian Movements in Britain and Ireland 1918–1945.*[1] Moreover, Kaiser engages fundamentally with the social question. His main work in this regard is to be found in the edited volume *Marx Viewed from the Right*, where he writes about the anti-capitalist tradition within the New Right, as well as about the possibility of creating an alliance between Left and Right — what he calls the "transverse front" (*Querfront*). Such issues have preoccupied him by virtue of his concern for the social question, which he considers of paramount importance for the Right if it is to avoid a conclusive fall into asocial liberalism.

---

1 Benedikt Kaiser and Eric Fröhlich, *Phänomen Inselfaschismus: Blackshirts, Blueshirts und weitere autoritäre Bewegungen in Großbritannien und Irland 1918–1945* (Regin-Verlag, 2013).

In the volume *Querfront*, part of the *Kaplaken* book series, Kaiser demonstrates that no effective political transverse front in history ever resulted from political cooperation between the Left and the Right. Rather, it emerged from an interaction of apparently contradictory ideological positions. He reaches this conclusion upon analyzing the following areas of concern: the EU, anti-capitalism from the Right, and capitalism as the driving force behind the Great Replacement, which makes an intellectual transverse front more necessary than ever today. In the process, he indicates that understanding the Great Replacement as a project of the century executed by people indoctrinated by red-green ideology conceals both the economic dimension and the imperialistic driving forces (Western war missions and regime changes) responsible for successive waves of refugees and migrants. While the blind spot of the Left lies in ignoring the national question, the Right's blind spot lies in their neglect of economic and foreign policy implications, which are more causally linked as the driving forces of mass immigration than Islam or multiculturalism.[2]

The young political scientist dares to throw another "look towards the left" in his contribution to the *Kaplaken* series. Here once again, he looks to the Left for potential opportunities to establish a transverse front. Quoting the late author Norbert Borrmann (1953–2016), Kaiser sees contemporary liberalism as the interplay of capital and left-wing ideology. This consists in a left-wing superstructure and a capitalist base. Such a seemingly contradictory alliance is possible only due to the shared philosophical origin between the Left and capital, which has its root in the Enlightenment and makes their collaboration mutually profitable.[3] The commodification of the fight against the Right, cultural diversity, and gender enables the Left to shape the superstructure of society. As Guillaume Paolis has observed, this

---

2   Benedikt Kaiser, *Querfront* (Schnellroda: Antaios, 2017), 67–88.

3   Benedikt Kaiser, *Blick nach Links* (Schnellroda: Antaios, 2019), 6.

leads to the side effects of capitalism becoming the hobbyhorse of the Left. As a result, Kaiser writes, a hypermoral feel-good program comes to take the place of a well-founded critique of capitalism for the benefit of the majority. This, Hannes Hofbauer argues, is why capital can so uncompromisingly identify itself with commitments to (sub-)cultural and sexual identities.[4]

The prevailing open borders policy in the West enables unchecked capitalist domination and uncontrolled investment activity. The profits thereby generated eventually accumulate in metropolitan areas. This is because, while the Left pursues socio-political hegemony, power politics are determined by capital. Therefore, the main force behind mass immigration is capital in the form of industrial and entrepreneurial associations. While, in Germany, this role is taken on by the Federation of German Industries (*Bundesverband der Deutschen Industrie*), in Austria this falls under the umbrella of the Federation of Austrian Industry (*Industriellenvereinigung*), both of which have a vested interest in fighting the Right. The motivation of capital consists in the suppression of wages and the elimination of the shortage in skilled workers, behind which, in turn, stands the ideology of liberalism with its dogma of a borderless world and a free market.[5] Instead of focusing on addressing economic inequality, the contemporary Left is fixated on minority identity politics. By pitting minorities against the beleaguered majority, the Left destroys community and carries the demands of liberalism to extremes. As such, both advocates of neoliberalism and Antifa members share the individual as their common purpose, which they intend to liberate from its oppression at the hands of the national collective.[6] The Right must bear in mind this congruence of interests between leftists and liberals whenever they flirt with the idea of an alliance with the former. After

---

4   Ibid., 7–8.

5   Ibid., 11–12.

6   Ibid., 13–14.

all, family, peoplehood, and statehood are pillars constituting the frontline of resistance for the two most important reference points of the 21st century: solidarity and identity.[7]

Standing in the tradition of the *Kaplaken* book series, Kaiser even sees potential for a transverse front (*Querfront*) with the two left-wing populist thinkers Chantal Mouffe and Ernesto Laclau, in antithesis to the liberal Left. In this regard, Kaiser makes an appeal to the category of the Political, which Mouffe and Laclau recognize. In this sense, their theory posits a front between the losers of globalization and those left behind, the so-called subalterns, whom they mobilize against the elites. In the thinking of Mouffe and Laclau, the people do not constitute a historically developed community, but are rather, as in Antonio Gramsci's thought, a popular alliance which unites people in a so-called "chain of equivalences" across ethnic and social boundaries with a common political purpose.[8] This concept of the people is a purely will-based one, which provides the basis for a radical socialist and democratic concept. By reformulating socialist ideals, a radical and plural democracy may emerge. In their anti-capitalist demands, Mouffe and Laclau insist on the abolition of the capitalist relations of production while nonetheless admitting that this would not equate to the total abolition of injustice. By restoring popular sovereignty, the people would finally regain their rights as they resist globalization.[9] Therefore, one of the main points of left-wing populism is the reappropriation of myth in the sense intended by Georges Sorel: the mobilizing image which appeases socialist ideas and pluralistic democracy with a new "going-to-the-people" approach, all while admitting the political competitors (the Right) as interlocutors.[10]

---

7   Ibid., 21.

8   Ibid., 42.

9   Ibid., 44.

10   Ibid., 44–45.

Following in the tradition of Carl Schmitt, Chantal Mouffe rejects the pursuit of political consensus and the denial of thinking in terms of the friend-enemy distinction, as he considers such an approach to be apolitical.[11] A mobilization of the people first requires their politicization, and this cannot be done without a conflictual representation of the world and a division into opposing camps with which people can identify.[12] The gap which Kaiser perceives on the Left is the lack of reference to a historically developed peoplehood. As a result, in the era of globalization, addressing the question of identity has become more pressing than ever. Overall, Kaiser sees the Left as incapable of using the current crises, which is not least due to their intellectuals being embedded in the workings of the left-liberal establishment. Instead of providing answers to Germans' need for identity in the face of globalization, the Left reacts like a petulant child, refusing to deal with the subject. Only a few exceptional figures, like Sarah Wagenknecht or, on the theoretical level, Chantal Mouffe, would oppose this, but they are constantly marginalized by their own camp. Ultimately, this syndrome will lead to a paralysis of the Left, since anyone could join the transverse front (*Querfront*) at a moment's notice. Thus, it would be a big mistake for the Right to seek concessions from left-liberal circles, for such a thing can never happen. However, a rapprochement with the Left would allow the Right to finally address the social question, thereby rendering the liberal Left superfluous. Only organic communities can provide social support to their members. According to Kaiser, societies that define themselves as borderless are incapable of doing so, hence the social experiments of the Left, which presuppose the acceptance of a multicultural society, cannot offer an alternative here.[13]

---

11   Ibid., 45.

12   Ibid., 46.

13   Ibid., 36–37.

Felix Menzel, born in 1985, is another protagonist of the New Right in Germany. As co-founder of the school newspaper *Blue Daffodil* [*Blaue Narzisse*] established in Chemnitz in 2004, Menzel has engaged with "controversial issues of politics, culture, historiography, and youth." Up until 2015, the authors of this publication released pamphlets concerning issues salient to the New Right, such as globalization and European unification; these texts are not only well thought-out, but also bear provocative cover pictures, such as that of the December 2008 issue, which bears the caption "The Federal Government informs us: Only 31 years remain until the death of the people." *Blue Daffodil* has recently been converted from a print magazine into an online blog in the wall-newspaper format, and it regularly publishes a section entitled "Instigations" (*Anstöße*), a series of publications with individual contributions on topics such as geopolitics, Europe (see the "Young Europe Instigation" written by Philip Stein and Felix Menzel), mass immigration, strategy debates, and general approaches to politics. In addition, Menzel runs the think tank *Recherche Dresden*, founded in 2018, with which he publishes the magazine *Recherche D*, a unique project on the German New Right that deals with economic issues and theories from the Right. The institute busies itself with the development of concepts for the time after the collapse of "global capitalism financed by monetary socialism," and advocates "in a publicist and political manner as well as in an advisory capacity for the preservation of what has developed historically and for the development of theoretical and practical alternatives to globalism." At the same time, *Recherche Dresden* raises the question of compatibility between, on the one hand, a free economic order that permits the individual, the family, the village, and the nation to operate in an economically free fashion, and, on the other hand, the preservation of community and the environment.[14] In 2018,

---

14 Recherche Dresden, *"Unserer Arbeit"* [https://recherche-dresden.de/unsere-arbeit/#1530614974486-79ccc147-3828].

Menzel published a study on the subject of "securing skilled workers without mass immigration."

In his 2009 *Kaplaken* volume *Media Rituals and Political Icons*, Menzel calls on the New Right to create new icons that capture and reflect the content of their own worldview in pictures.[15] Only through these key images can people form a picture of a political movement. In his *Kaplaken* volume concentrated on media theory, Menzel indicates that the images of reality presented by the media are merely constructs; consequently, it is important to question and deconstruct narratives that depict an illusion rather than genuine *Being* (*das Sein*). It is particularly important to critique such narrative-images, Menzel argues, because the myths and ritualised forms presented in the media are detached from real life. By means of illusory historical claims and "humanitarian" talking points, people in Germany are distracted from real problems.[16] However, real community-building can only occur through the production of media materials that are more faithful to real life, and which can arm the people and nation with the necessary symbols.[17] Based on, and in response to, Antonio Gramsci, Menzel insists that the patriotic camp must take up the fight for the "pre-political" (*vorpolitisch*) space and symbolic power. Hence, we must not only tend to the political, but also to high and popular culture. The main obstacle here would be to prove that the mass media, acting as gatekeepers of information and deciding what gets reported, which nowadays is practically equivalent to deciding whether events happened or not.[18] But the Internet 2.0 provides the space for individuals to participate in the creation of texts, videos, and images. The aim of this operation must be to make individual contributions go viral and bring the message to the masses

---

15   Felix Menzel, *Medienrituale und politische Ikonen* (Antaios, 2009), 93.

16   Ibid., 86.

17   Ibid., 87.

18   Ibid., 89.

through aggressive marketing. Via forums, social networks, and communities, the gatekeepers can be bypassed, and subversive messages can be disseminated — a practice that proved increasingly difficult during the arbitrary censorship regimes of social media sites like Facebook, Twitter, and YouTube; but, now, in the era of X, the options for such dissemination are growing. Amateur photography, film making, and journalism can be employed to ensure the viral spread of an intended political message. It is important to generate key images that reflect the movement's worldview and to develop representative, charismatic figures who mirror this point of view.[19] These key images can be created by activists who make their own activity into a media image. Thus, Menzel has responded to Kubitschek's challenge and articulated a theory of right-wing activism which is fundamentally relevant today and will shape the near future.

---

19   Ibid., 91.

The Rise of the New Right

S INCE THE birth of the New Right in France, even before that
of the New Left in the Summer of 1968, a revolutionary pan-
European school of thought has come into being, one that has explicitly articulated itself as a rejection of the Old Right. From the very
beginning, it has identified liberalism as the main enemy and has
striven for a cultural revolution from the Right to overcome it. Its
intellectual roots can be traced back to the Conservative Revolution,
which emerged towards the end of the 19th century as a reaction to
liberalism, and also to the writings of two national-revolutionaries:
Dominique Venner and Jean Thiriart. The most important idea of
this revolution is that it does not view parliamentarism as the intended purpose of metapolitics. Rather, it sees in parliamentarism
nothing more than the implementation of shifts in thinking which
have already taken place in the mind. Thus, the real purpose of action consists in articulating and disseminating new thoughts and
concepts which enable an intellectual revolution and the overcoming
of liberalism.

In the spirit of ethnopluralism initially imported from Germany,
the New Right advocates for the diversity of peoples and the preservation of different ethnic groups, religions, and civilizations. By
the same token, it opposes racism, colonialism, and the Western
superiority complex, all of which were present in the Old Right and
which are currently aspects of liberalism in its universalist preten-
sions. Originally designated as *Nouvelle Culture* (New Culture),
the New Right follows in the spirit of Oswald Spengler in seeking a

new beginning for Europe, opposing the old Western civilization that has ossified in its materialism and the artificial culture of the Enlightenment. By rejecting the West's claim to universality, the New Right understands European civilization to be only one among many civilizations, and believes that Europeans share a common struggle with Africa and Asia against Americanization and globalization. In doing so, the New Right does not stop at the anti-imperialism of the Left, but strives to establish an intellectual "cross-front" (*Querfront*) that engages numerous left-wing subjects from right-wing perspectives. This includes not only the reception of Antonio Gramsci and his theory of cultural hegemony, but also a fundamental critique of capitalism. By orienting itself towards the esoteric Karl Marx and his understanding of capitalism as a system aimed at the domination of things (as well as Aristotle's critique of money), the New Right not only questions particular aspects of capitalism, such as the the interest-debt system, but is against the whole essence of the economic system in its aiming for infinite growth. The New Right sees a possible alternative in the critique of growth, which not only questions the capitalistic drive, but also the calls for infinite extension, expansion, and destruction (of human communities and the environment) that are inherent in any growth-based economy.

While today's globalist Left calls for an end to the nation-state in order to aid the dawning of an all-levelling world state, the New Right recognizes the need for a European *Imperium* that preserves diverse identities, be they regional, national, or civilizational (in the sense of a culture group), and safeguards them from globalization. In this regard, today's nation-state is rendered helpless, incapable of asserting the multiple levels of identity or preserving the people, and instead slated to further serve the agenda of globalization and contributing to the levelling process. This applies to both natives and immigrants. In bourgeois society, the New Right sees nothing worth preserving, only a problem, because such a society insidiously destroys all communities through its unrelenting propaganda of individualism and assaults on personality, transforming all personal and collective ties into one sellable and negotiable value. In contrast, the New Right calls for the restoration of historically developed communities and the replacement of the modern individual by the premodern person.

Since its inception, the New Right has continued to develop and sharpen its profile. Not all actors and intellectuals associated with it have followed this path; some have gone their own way. Guillaume Faye, a prodigious *alumnus* of the New Right, is one such figure. Starting with his book *Archeofuturism*, Faye critiqued the New Right for its solidarity with the Third World, its ethnopluralism, and its aversion to the United States and modernity. Such "right-wingers" do not live up to the tradition of the New Right, but rather are, at best, a "new Right" in the sense of a newly emerging direction on the Right which sees Islam and mass immigration, rather than liberalism, as Europe's main enemies. In a step backwards to the Old Right, they assert the supremacy of Western civilization above all other civilizations and spread the fairy-tale of their "Judeo-Christian" heritage, obliging Europeans to stand in unconditional solidarity with Zionism. Through this mechanism, the correlations with Western wars and coups in the Middle East are elided, and the logic of the Cold War is being revived. In the most extreme cases, Russia and China are designated as totalitarian enemies of Western freedom to be ruthlessly fought.

Although Faye's notion of "archeofuturism" proposes a union of tradition and modernity, it becomes clear upon closer inspection that his ultimate goal is a hypermodernity leading to phenomena such as human cloning and cyborgs. In these circles, the necessary solidarity of all "White" peoples is invoked in contrast to Islam, which in turn is depicted with the most demonic traits, accused of civilizational "backwardness" and of belonging to a unified bloc. Taking up such a view, one turns a blind eye to the major differences within Islam (Shiites, Sunnis, Sufis, Wahhabis) and completely negates the Western support for Islamists in the likes of the Islamic State or al-Qaeda. To paraphrase Alain Soral, we are dealing with people who shout, "Don't Islamicize our Americanization!" Unlike Renaud Camus, these people do not bear in mind the fact that demographic replacement is only possible when a people has been entirely decomposed by individualism and no longer possesses any awareness of its roots, religion, or culture. Accordingly, the liberal decomposition of feminism, LGBT rights, and individualism are defended tooth and nail as if part of European culture against supposed Islamization.

In the words of Daniel Friberg, one can describe these people as representatives of the "false Right" or "imposter Right," representing nothing more than a convenient pseudo-alternative to the ideas of the New Right. Serving their function as gatekeepers for the liberal system and critiquing the lines of argumentation is their order of the day. According to Huntington's *Clash of Civilizations*, this logic leads to the illusion that Europe is trapped on the geopolitical chessboard between a liberal right-wing of the Donald Trump variety—pro-capitalist, anti-Islamic, pro-Zionist, and pro-American—and a liberal left-wing which advocates globalism and wishes to bulldoze all peoples and religions on its way towards a liberal world-state. At the present moment, representatives of the Clash of Civilizations and right-wing liberalism still dominate the discussion on the Right, but the ideas of the New Right are gaining in circulation and enjoying engagement from increasingly more followers. This is critical: given the illusory choice between neo-Western right-wing liberalism and globalist left-wing Liberalism, neither of these sides is correct, and neither side offers a geopolitical vision for Europe.

A solution for Europe can be found in Alexander Dugin's concept of the Fourth Political Theory, which synthesizes the ideas of the New Right with his own Eurasian project, within which Russia and Western Europe are to become intimately linked. By returning to its own tradition and Christian roots, Eurasia will open the door to a positive future. Meanwhile, the West faces the prospect of being reduced to a US-centered civilization confined within the precepts of the original Monroe Doctrine and incapable of enforcing the doctrines of human rights, capitalism, and liberalism in Europe, Africa, or China.

Will the emerging multipolar world be without conflicts or clashes? No. But, by finally recollecting our identity and refraining from imposing it on others, we Europeans will finally be able to channel our energies not only in drafting our own legislation and reviving our traditions, but also in permitting other nations to define their own destiny. Only then can we understand that the multiplicity of Daseins and the fascinating pluriverse, with its myriad languages, tribes, and ways of life, is the true treasure of mankind — not the cold, utterly rationalized Western civilization with its worldview centered around profits, lack of limitations, and violence. Alexander Dugin's ethnosociology as well as his studies in the War of Ideas (*Noomakhia*) present a first attempt at truly understanding the peoples of the world, a chance to reach an understanding between peoples on a more equal footing. In the end, it is up to each and every one of us to bring this about, whether we as Europeans succeed in becoming masters of ourselves once more, or whether we press on into the abyss of Western postmodernism.

OTHER BOOKS PUBLISHED BY ARKTOS

Virginia Abernethy — *Born Abroad*

Sri Dharma Pravartaka Acharya — *The Dharma Manifesto*

Joakim Andersen — *Rising from the Ruins*

Karl-Olov Arnstberg — *The Sweden Syndrome*

Winston C. Banks — *Excessive Immigration*

Stephen Baskerville — *Who Lost America?*

Alfred Baeumler — *Nietzsche: Philosopher and Politician*

Matt Battaglioli — *The Consequences of Equality*

Alain de Benoist — *Beyond Human Rights*
Carl Schmitt Today
The Ideology of Sameness
The Indo-Europeans
Manifesto for a European Renaissance
On the Brink of the Abyss
The Problem of Democracy
Runes and the Origins of Writing
View from the Right (vol. 1–3)

Armand Berger — *Tolkien, Europe, and Tradition*

Pawel Bielawski — *European Apostasy*

Arthur Moeller van den Bruck — *Germany's Third Empire*

Kerry Bolton — *The Perversion of Normality*
Revolution from Above
Yockey: A Fascist Odyssey

Isac Boman — *Money Power*

Daniel Branco — *The Absolute Philosopher*

Charles William Dailey — *The Serpent Symbol in Tradition*

Antoine Dresse — *Political Realism*

Ricardo Duchesne — *Faustian Man in a Multicultural Age*

Alexander Dugin — *Ethnos and Society*
Ethnosociology
Eurasian Mission
The Fourth Political Theory
The Great Awakening vs the Great Reset
Last War of the World-Island
Politica Aeterna
Political Platonism
Putin vs Putin
The Rise of the Fourth Political Theory
The Trump Revolution
Templars of the Proletariat
The Theory of a Multipolar World

Daria Dugina — *A Theory of Europe*

Edward Dutton — *Race Differences in Ethnocentrism*

Mark Dyal — *Hated and Proud*

Clare Ellis — *The Blackening of Europe* (vol. 1–3)

Koenraad Elst — *Return of the Swastika*

Julius Evola — *The Bow and the Club*
Fascism Viewed from the Right
A Handbook for Right-Wing Youth
Metaphysics of Power
Metaphysics of War

OTHER BOOKS PUBLISHED BY ARKTOS

	The Myth of the Blood
	Notes on the Third Reich
	Pagan Imperialism
	Recognitions
	A Traditionalist Confronts Fascism
GUILLAUME FAYE	*Against Russophobia*
	Archeofuturism
	Archeofuturism 2.0
	The Colonisation of Europe
	Convergence of Catastrophes
	Ethnic Apocalypse
	A Global Coup
	Prelude to War
	Sex and Deviance
	Understanding Islam
	Why We Fight
DANIEL S. FORREST	*Suprahumanism*
ANDREW FRASER	*Dissident Dispatches*
	Reinventing Aristocracy in the Age of Woke Capital
	The WASP Question
GÉNÉRATION IDENTITAIRE	*We are Generation Identity*
PETER GOODCHILD	*The Taxi Driver from Baghdad*
	The Western Path
PAUL GOTTFRIED	*War and Democracy*
GEORGES GUISCARD	*White Privilege*
LAURENT GUYÉNOT	*The Papal Curse*
PETR HAMPL	*Breached Enclosure*
PORUS HOMI HAVEWALA	*The Saga of the Aryan Race*
CONSTANTIN VON HOFFMEISTER	*Esoteric Trumpism*
	MULTIPOLARITY!
RICHARD HOUCK	*Liberalism Unmasked*
A. J. ILLINGWORTH	*Political Justice*
INSTITUT ILIADE	*For a European Awakening*
	Guardians of Heritage
ALEXANDER JACOB	*De Naturae Natura*
JASON REZA JORJANI	*Artemis Unveiled*
	Closer Encounters
	Erosophia
	Faustian Futurist
	Iranian Leviathan
	Lovers of Sophia
	Metapolemos
	Novel Folklore
	Philosophy of the Future
	Prometheism
	Promethean Pirate
	Prometheus and Atlas
	Psychotron
	Thanosis
	Uber Man
	World State of Emergency
HENRIK JONASSON	*Sigmund*
EDGAR JULIUS JUNG	*The Significance of the German Revolution*

OTHER BOOKS PUBLISHED BY ARKTOS

RUUBEN KAALEP & AUGUST MEISTER — *Rebirth of Europe*

LANCE KENNEDY — *The Book of the Scribe*

JAMES KIRKPATRICK — *Conservatism Inc.*

LUDWIG KLAGES — *The Biocentric Worldview*
Cosmogonic Reflections
The Science of Character

ANDREW KORYBKO — *Hybrid Wars*

PIERRE KREBS — *Guillaume Faye: Truths & Tributes*
Fighting for the Essence

JULIEN LANGELLA — *Catholic and Identitarian*

HENRI LEVAVASSEUR — *Identity: The Foundation of the City*

JOHN BRUCE LEONARD — *The New Prometheans*

DIANA PANCHENKO — *The Inevitable*

JEAN-YVES LE GALLOU — *The Propaganda Society*

STEPHEN PAX LEONARD — *The Ideology of Failure*
Travels in Cultural Nihilism

WILLIAM S. LIND — *Reforging Excalibur*
Retroculture

PENTTI LINKOLA — *Can Life Prevail?*

GIORGIO LOCCHI — *Definitions*

H. P. LOVECRAFT — *The Conservative*

NORMAN LOWELL — *Imperium Europa*

RICHARD LYNN — *Sex Differences in Intelligence*
A Tribute to Helmut Nyborg (ed.)

JOHN MACLUGASH — *The Return of the Solar King*

CHARLES MAURRAS — *The Future of the Intelligentsia &*
For a French Awakening

GRAEME MAXTON — *The Follies of the Western Mind*

JOHN HARMON MCELROY — *Agitprop in America*

MICHAEL O'MEARA — *Guillaume Faye and the Battle of Europe*
New Culture, New Right

MICHAEL MILLERMAN — *Beginning with Heidegger*

DMITRY MOISEEV — *The Philosophy of Italian Fascism*

MAURICE MURET — *The Greatness of Elites*

BRIAN ANSE PATRICK — *The NRA and the Media*
Rise of the Anti-Media
The Ten Commandments of Propaganda
Zombology

TITO PERDUE — *The Bent Pyramid*
Journey to a Location
Lee
Morning Crafts
Philip
The Sweet-Scented Manuscript
William's House (vol. 1–4)

JOHN K. PRESS — *A Call to Arts*
The True West vs the Zombie Apocalypse

RAIDO — *A Handbook of Traditional Living (vol. 1–2)*

P R REDDALL — *Towards Awakening*

OTHER BOOKS PUBLISHED BY ARKTOS

CLAIRE RAE RANDALL	*The War on Gender*
STEVEN J. ROSEN	*The Agni and the Ecstasy*
	The Jedi in the Lotus
NICHOLAS ROONEY	*Talking to the Wolf*
RICHARD RUDGLEY	*Barbarians*
	Essential Substances
	Wildest Dreams
ERNST VON SALOMON	*It Cannot Be Stormed*
	The Outlaws
WERNER SOMBART	*Traders and Heroes*
PIERO SAN GIORGIO	*Giuseppe*
	Survive the Economic Collapse
	Surviving the Next Catastrophe
SRI SRI RAVI SHANKAR	*Celebrating Silence*
	Know Your Child
	Management Mantras
	Patanjali Yoga Sutras
	Secrets of Relationships
OSWALD SPENGLER	*The Decline of the West*
	Man and Technics
RICHARD STOREY	*The Uniqueness of Western Law*
J. R. SOMMER	*The New Colossus*
TOMISLAV SUNIC	*Against Democracy and Equality*
	Homo Americanus
	Postmortem Report
	Titans are in Town
ASKR SVARTE	*Gods in the Abyss*
HANS-JÜRGEN SYBERBERG	*On the Fortunes and Misfortunes of Art in Post-War Germany*
ABIR TAHA	*Defining Terrorism*
	The Epic of Arya (2nd ed.)
	Nietzsche is Coming God, or the Redemption of the Divine
	Verses of Light
JEAN THIRIART	*Europe: An Empire of 400 Million*
BAL GANGADHAR TILAK	*The Arctic Home in the Vedas*
BOSTIAN MARCO TURK	*War in the Name of Peace*
DOMINIQUE VENNER	*Ernst Jünger: A Different European Destiny*
	For a Positive Critique
	The Shock of History
HANS VOGEL	*How Europe Became American*
TIM VORGENS	*Legitimate Preference*
WELTANSCHAUUNG ITALIA	*From Nihilism to Transcendence*
MARKUS WILLINGER	*A Europe of Nations*
	Generation Identity
ALEXANDER WOLFHEZE	*Alba Rosa*
	Globus Horribilis
	Rupes Nigra